THE
EASY VEGAN
COOKBOOK

Make Healthy Home Cooking Practically Effortless

KATHY HESTER

bestselling author of
The Great Vegan Bean Book and *OATrageous Oatmeals*

PAGE STREET
PUBLISHING CO.

PAGE STREET
PUBLISHING CO.

Copyright © 2015 Kathy Hester

First published in 2015 by

Page Street Publishing Co.

27 Congress Street, Suite 105

Salem, MA 01970

www.pagestreetpublishing.com

Distributed by Macmillan; sales in Canada by The Canadian Manda Group.

19   18   5   6   7   8

ISBN-13: 978-1-62414-147-8

ISBN-10: 1-62414-147-1

Library of Congress Control Number: 2015930605

Cover and book design by Page Street Publishing Co.

Photography by Ann Oliverio

Printed and bound in China

THIS BOOK WOULDN'T BE POSSIBLE
WITHOUT MY SUPPORT SYSTEM OF READERS,
TESTERS, BLOGGERS, FRIENDS AND AGENTS.
THIS BOOK IS FOR ALL OF YOU!

CONTENTS

CHAPTER 3
SIMPLE STEWS 61

CHAPTER 4
PUSHOVER PASTAS 83

CHAPTER 5
MANAGEABLE MAINS 105

CHAPTER 6
SPEEDY STIR-FRIES 129

CHAPTER 7
EASY SANDWICH FILLINGS AND SPREADS 141

CHAPTER 8
STRAIGHT-FORWARD SIDES 161

CHAPTER 9

DESSERTS AND DRINKS 177

INTRODUCTION

In this book you'll find tips, ideas and recipes to help make every dinner you cook a more pleasant and easier experience—even after one of "those" days.

Personally, I find it easy to get excited about cooking for a big dinner party for friends, but harder when it's just Tuesday night dinner—again.

We all need to remember that it's okay to make things easier. I don't know about you, but I tend to be an overachiever. The word "easy" often makes me feel like I'm not doing enough; but, when you get right down to it, there's not much difference between eating a dinner that you worked on for 20 minutes and eating a dinner that you prepped for eight hours. If dinner is the only goal of the evening, it's not necessary to wear yourself out planning and making it.

Most of the recipes in this book can be put together fairly quickly. Some will have cooking times of up to an hour or so, but that includes hands-off time during which you can do household chores, watch TV, hang with your kids, or just read a book and have a glass of wine.

Try to remember that a recipe typically takes more time when you first make it. And, if you're new to cooking, it will take a little longer to break down and cut up veggies. Don't worry, you'll speed up in no time. We all started there.

SPECIAL DIETS AND NUTRITIONAL INFORMATION

I try to make my recipes adaptable for as many diets as possible. Almost all of these recipes can be made gluten-free, soy-free and/or without oil. I give substitutes if the original recipe includes something you'd rather leave out.

I will specify soy milk for the biscuit recipes, but they come out great with almond or coconut milk, too. However, only soy milk curdles like buttermilk, so that's why it's my first choice.

Feel free to use these recipes as a starting place, and change them to suit your needs and tastes. I never follow a recipe exactly, and I don't expect you to either!

The nutritional information is provided as a "ballpark" figure, so if you have a medical condition that requires you to keep strict track, I encourage you to enter the recipes into the nutritional calculator recommended by your doctor.

Here's why the nutritional information I provide may differ from yours when you make a recipe at home:

- The recipe options differ in nutritional value and calories.

- Nutritional content of certain products varies among brands.

- Nondairy milks vary widely, and if you use plain in place of unsweetened, the difference can be significant.

- Nutritional information is calculated on each recipe as written, using unsweetened almond milk as the default nondairy milk. If there is a range in the amounts, such as "1 to 2 tablespoons olive oil," the lower amount is used for calculation.

TO PLAN MEALS OR NOT TO PLAN MEALS

It's true that being organized makes life easier, and with cooking it's no different. But I will be the first to admit that I skip planning when my life gets hectic.

The main advantage of writing up a meal plan every week is that those 30 minutes of planning can result in your having to make only one shopping trip instead of multiple trips. That can be hours saved, especially if you usually go after work when the stores are crowded.

The disadvantage is that planning commits you to eating specific meals during the week, and for some households that just doesn't work. Cheryl, my picky eater, can come home with a craving that my plan didn't include. One solution is to plan with one day open for a meal from the freezer or pantry.

Even if you do plan meticulously, you'll still want to keep your pantry and freezer stocked so you don't go hunting all over for tomato paste or the last of the brown rice. But some days the rice will be in your shopping bag where you left it in the hall after the dogs had a meltdown the moment you walked in the door. (Not that that ever happens in my house!)

Don't forget to think outside the box when you don't have every ingredient called for in a recipe. You can substitute sweet potato for butternut squash, collards for kale, cooked rice for cooked pasta. All these substitutions are simple to do and work out great. Use seasonal vegetables whenever possible.

I'm not going to tell you there's any one way to cook every day or that you must plan meals. You know what fits best into your life. But if you're looking for a few ideas to grease your routine, you're in the right place.

One easy trick I use when life gets crazy is planning a certain type of food for each night, though without a specific recipe. This method leaves my plan open enough that I can use up all those turnips from my CSA (community supported agriculture) box or the last of the black beans. If I let Cheryl know, she can even start craving it before she comes home. For example:

MONDAY: stir-fry

TUESDAY: pasta

WEDNESDAY: Mexican

THURSDAY: tofu, tempeh or seitan

FRIDAY: slow cooker soup or stew

You can save time during preparation, too. Hate the thought of cutting onions and prepping veggies night after night? Take one or two nights a week to prep so that, when you come home, all you have to do is cook. You can freeze chopped, uncooked onions and green peppers in the portion sizes you'll need. It's nice to have a happy surprise on a day that you need to get dinner on the table quickly.

Prepping ahead can also cut down on food waste. I used to convince myself that I would use everything from my CSA, but I ended up with leftovers that were too far gone to freeze by the time I got to them. Now I wash, dry and break down my greens and store them in the refrigerator in sealed containers, each packed with a paper towel to maintain freshness. The greens are then ready to throw in a stir-fry or stew, and I can easily freeze what I don't use. If I do this consistently, I can always pull prepped greens from the freezer if I find I underestimated the amount I have in the refrigerator.

USE YOUR FREEZER FOR THE POWER OF GOOD

I think of my freezer as an extension of my pantry. When I want to make, say, broccoli with garlic sauce, I pull a bag of broccoli out of the freezer to go with my sauce ingredients. With a few bags of frozen veggies on hand, I can save on prep time and I won't be tempted to overspend on take out food or make extra trips to the store.

Be sure to check out Stocking Your Pantry in the resources section on page 198. It will give you an idea of what nonfreezer items to have on hand. There is also a spice list you can use to build your collection spice by spice and still stay on your budget.

Below I talk about freezing your own veggies, but I like to keep some store-bought frozen vegetables on hand, too. Many organic frozen vegetables are cheaper than fresh organic ones. Remember, there is no shame in using store-bought frozen vegetables. They are often fresher than the organics in your local grocery.

FREEZE YOUR OWN VEGGIES

Onions, peppers and greens are great to prep and store in the freezer. But what about other veggies?

You don't want to freeze veggies that have lots of liquid in them—the ones you would pick from your garden before a frost. There is a little leeway, but lettuce and other watery leaves don't do well in the freezer. Greens are the exception, but you'll want to cook them a little first and drain them well before tossing them in the freezer in freezer bags or freezer-safe containers.

Beets, sweet potatoes, winter squash, green beans, cooked beans, anything from the cabbage family (cauliflower, cabbage, broccoli), carrots and peas—all these freeze well. If you see it in the freezer section of your grocer, then there's a great chance you can freeze it, too.

Many vegetables need to be blanched in boiling water for a certain amount of time, then rinsed with cool water, before freezing. Check your local food preservation website or agriculture extension to get detailed freezing and preserving information for every vegetable you want to freeze.

Cooked potatoes develop a grainy texture in the freezer, but you can blanch cubes or cut them into fry shapes and toss them in the freezer. I do freeze some soups that have a little potato in them, but I wouldn't freeze a soup that included potato as a main ingredient.

Another way to have your own back is to premake some staples or whole meals so they are ready to go straight from the freezer. A frozen lasagna or a batch of maple walnut vegan sausage patties can save you from driving to the store or just giving up and going out to eat.

Remember: If you use frozen ingredients straight from the freezer, your meal will need a longer cooking time. You can thaw ingredients by tossing them in the refrigerator the night before or even in your microwave in a pinch.

If you belong to a CSA, or if you fall in love with something at the farmers' market, you may end up with more of an ingredient than you can use before it goes bad. This is the best time to start freezing.

WHAT TO ALWAYS HAVE IN YOUR FREEZER

When you think of your freezer as part of your pantry, you need to consider what you should always keep there. I keep mine stocked with vegetables that I use often. They can be store-bought, homemade or a combination of the two.

In addition to plain frozen vegetables, I always have a bag of French fries made of potatoes or sweet potatoes and at least one lasagna or casserole.

FREEZER "PANTRY" LIST

- ✔ chopped onion (not blanched; just chopped and frozen)
- ✔ chopped bell pepper (also not blanched; just chopped and frozen)
- ✔ pre-sautéed mushrooms
- ✔ broccoli florets or peeled, chopped stalks
- ✔ cauliflower florets
- ✔ green beans: French, Italian and regular
- ✔ kale, collards or other greens, quickly blanched and drained well
- ✔ California mix (carrots, broccoli and cauliflower)
- ✔ Italian mix (cauliflower, broccoli, zucchini, Italian green beans, red peppers, carrots and lima beans)
- ✔ Asian blend (green beans, broccoli, carrots, red pepper, onions and mushrooms)
- ✔ mixed vegetables (corn, carrots, green beans and peas; and sometimes I add edamame)
- ✔ frozen precooked beans in 1½- or 3-cup bags (the equivalent of 1 or 2 15-oz [439-g] cans)
- ✔ frozen precooked tomatoes and tomato sauce in 1½- or 3-cup (240-480 g) baggies
- ✔ winter squash (including pumpkin): blanched cubes and purée
- ✔ veggie burgers—store-bought or homemade
- ✔ French fries or sweet potato fries
- ✔ frozen rolls or half a loaf of bread or bread dough
- ✔ homemade biscuits (precooked if drop biscuits, but use raw dough with waxed paper between them if they are rolled biscuits)
- ✔ homemade pizza dough

CHAPTER 1

MAKE-AHEAD STAPLES

I love making my own staples, and I think you will, too. When you make them at home instead of buying them, you know exactly what ingredients are used. There are no added preservatives or hidden ingredients that you have to check for.

Homemade bouillon and beans cooked from scratch can save you lots of money in the long run. The trick is to freeze some of the extra each time you make them, so that even on the busiest of nights you have some already on hand.

I have many other practical recipes for you like Almond Ricotta (page 24), delicious Maple Walnut Breakfast Sausage Patties (page 35) and Mushroom Red Pepper Pasta Sauce (page 85). You can double some of these and freeze them so you have enough for the whole month.

EASY HOMEMADE BOUILLON

• *gluten-free* • *soy-free* • *no oil added*

Store-bought veggie bouillon can be expensive, and it's hard to find exactly what I want. You'll be surprised at just how easy it is to make, and you can vary it with the veggies and herbs you have on hand. Making this is much easier than even reading all the ingredients on all the packages at the store.

MAKES ABOUT 3 CUPS (710 ML)

BASE INGREDIENTS

1 large onion, cut into quarters

3 large carrots

2 stalks celery

1 cup (87 g) mushrooms, optional (will create a beefy-flavored bouillon)

3 whole garlic cloves

2 teaspoons (10 g) dried thyme (or about ¼ cup [10 g] packed fresh)

1 teaspoon dried rosemary (or about 1 tablespoon [2.5 g] fresh)

ADDITIONS TO THE BASE INGREDIENTS (OPTIONAL)

1 to 2 teaspoons dried oregano

1 to 2 teaspoons dried marjoram

1 to 2 teaspoons dried basil

1 to 2 teaspoons dried thyme

1 to 2 teaspoons dried rosemary

1 to 2 teaspoons celery seed

1 to 2 teaspoons tarragon

2 bay leaves

A handful of fresh herbs

TO ADD AFTER COOKING (OPTIONAL)

½ cup (48 g) nutritional yeast (will create a chickeny-flavored bouillon)

Salt

Pepper

More fresh herbs

OVEN-COOKING METHOD

Preheat your oven to 350°F (177°C). Layer the base ingredients on the bottom of a Dutch oven and bake for about 1 hour, or until the veggies are soft. I do not roast them with water or oil, but you may certainly drizzle them with olive oil or use ¼ to ½ cup (59-118 ml) water. You could even top them with salt and pepper.

SLOW COOKER METHOD

Add the base ingredients to a 2- to 4-quart (2-4-L) slow cooker. (If you use a 4-quart [4-L] slow cooker or larger, add an additional ½ cup [118 ml] water). Cook on low while you are asleep or at work, about 8 to 9 hours. If you think you will cook the bouillon longer, or if your slow cooker runs hot, add ½ cup (118 ml) water. You can cook it on high for 3 to 4 hours if you prefer.

FINISHING THE BOUILLON, BOTH METHODS

Once the veggies are cooked, remove any tough herb stems that will not purée. Add the veggies to your food processor or a strong blender. This is the time to add salt, pepper, fresh herbs or nutritional yeast. The nutritional yeast adds another layer of depth and is my favorite addition.

Store in the refrigerator in a covered jar however much you think you will use in a week. Freeze the rest in ice-cube trays. Once the cubes are solid, remove them from the trays and store in a freezer bag. When measuring for a recipe, use twice as much of this bouillon as you would store-bought bouillon.

Per 1 cup (237 ml) serving: Calories 78.5, protein 2.2 g, total fat 0.0 g, carbohydrates 9.7 g, sodium 65.0 mg, fiber 3.0 g

DIY GOLDEN CREAMY GRAVY

• gluten-free option* • soy-free • no oil added

There was a time when I always made my gravy from a prepackaged vegan mix. It takes about the same amount of time to make your own, and it's dirt cheap. You can make a plain gravy to spoon over your garlic rosemary mashed potatoes or a jazzier one with herbs to pour over food that's simple.

MAKES ABOUT 3 CUPS (710 ML)

¼ cup (30g) flour (whole wheat or *brown rice flour)

2 cups (470 g) vegetable broth (or 2 cups [475 ml] water plus 1 vegetable bouillon cube)

2 cups (473 ml) unsweetened nondairy milk

2 tablespoons (10 g) nutritional yeast

Salt and pepper, to taste

EXTRAS, TO TASTE (OPTIONAL)

Thyme

Sage

Rosemary

Garlic powder

Onion powder

Heat a large sauté pan (enough to hold 4 cups [0.95 L] of liquid and still have a little room) over medium heat. Add the flour and sauté until it gets just a shade darker, about 3 to 4 minutes.

Slowly whisk in the broth about ½ cup (118 ml) at a time. Once it is incorporated, add ½ cup (118 ml) nondairy milk at a time, whisking constantly.

Turn the heat up to medium-high and let the sauce reduce and get thick. Whisk often. It will take about 20 to 30 minutes to thicken up. Once it's almost as thick as you'd like, take it off the heat and whisk in the nutritional yeast, salt and pepper plus any extra herbs you'd like to add in. It will continue to thicken until it cools.

Per 1 cup (237 ml) serving: Calories 83.8, protein 4.0 g, total fat 2.5 g, carbohydrates 12.0 g, sodium 500.0 mg, fiber 2.6 g

TIP: You can hurry this gravy along by turning the heat to high after all the milk is added. Keep on high until the mixture almost begins to boil, then lower the heat to medium-high. Be sure to watch it like a hawk and whisk often.

CAULIFLOWER MEXI MINCE

• *gluten-free* • *soy-free* • *no oil added*

Cheryl likes to eat a few hearty meals a week. She is not a vegan, but she agrees to eat vegan at home as long as I make some meat-like substitutions. Honestly, she would eat vegan mac and chez or store-bought vegan crispy fingers with ketchup every day. I like to make gluten- and soy-free versions of things like this mince so she gets what she wants and I get some extra veggies in her. Use this mince in burritos, tacos, pasta or anywhere else you'd like to try it out.

MAKES ABOUT 3 CUPS (688 G)

½ medium head of cauliflower, minced (about 4 cups [918 g])

2 teaspoons (10 g) cumin

2 teaspoons (10 g) oregano

1½ teaspoons (7 g) garlic powder (or 1 clove fresh, minced)

1 teaspoon coriander powder

1 teaspoon paprika

1 teaspoon salt

1 teaspoon of your favorite chili powder (I use ½ teaspoon ancho and ½ teaspoon jalapeño)

Preheat your oven to 350°F (177°C). Line two baking sheets with parchment paper.

Add all the ingredients to a mixing bowl and mix well. All of the spices should easily stick to the cauliflower bits.

Spread thinly on the baking sheets and bake for 10 minutes. Then stir and bake 10 more minutes.

Per ¼ cup (57 g) serving: Calories 8.7, protein 0.7 g, total fat 0.1 g, carbohydrates 1.7 g, sodium 10.0 mg, fiber 0.8 g

TIPS: Use a food processor to mince the cauliflower.

Try this with different spice combinations such as Italian to top a pizza, or even use the Maple Walnut Sausage Patties spices from the recipe on page 35 for an all-veggie homemade sausage.

PLAIN UNSWEETENED OAT MILK

• gluten-free option* • soy-free • no oil added

This recipe is from *OATrageous Oatmeals*. I'm including it in case you can't find unsweetened nondairy milk where you live. It's also nice to be able to make a batch on the fly instead of trekking out to the grocery store. Since you probably have oats on hand, you can make this on the spot. Oat milk is so easy to make; it's rich and creamy and much cheaper than store-bought.

MAKES 4 CUPS (946 ML)

4 cups (946 ml) water

1 cup (80 g) steel-cut oats or rolled oats (*make sure they are labeled "gluten-free")

Sweetener of choice to taste, optional

Add the water and oats to your blender and soak. If you are using steel-cut oats, soak for at least 30 minutes; if you are using rolled oats, soak for 10 minutes. Then blend for 1 to 2 minutes until smooth. Pour the oat mixture through a fine mesh strainer into a pitcher or a bowl with a spout. You will need to scrape the bottom of the strainer with a spoon when it gets clogged.

Remove the sediment from the strainer, rinse the blender and then strain one more time. You can strain back into the blender.

Now you have plain unsweetened oat milk!

This milk will keep for 3 to 4 days in the refrigerator. It will separate, but you can mix it in the blender to get it to come back together.

Per 1 cup (237 ml) serving with no pulp removed: Calories 140, protein 6.0 g, total fat 2.5 g, carbohydrates 27.0 g, sodium 0 mg, fiber 4.0 g

TIP: You can make other nondairy milks as well. Try soaked almonds, cashews, rice or coconut in place of the oats.

You will need to soak all of these longer to get the creamiest milk if your blender is not very powerful. I also recommend using a nut milk bag instead of a fine mesh strainer to get the best results. Otherwise, the milks will be slightly grainy.

VEGAN SOUR CREAM SUBSTITUTES

Here are two vegan sour cream substitutes. Both are gluten-free and one is soy-free. I hope one of these will fit your dietary needs. Both of these recipes make about 1 cup (118 ml) and can be used to thicken soups or stews, as a base for dips or as a topping for potatoes and burritos.

You may already have your own recipe for sour cream. Feel free to use it; it should work fine for this book.

CASHEW SOUR CREAM

• *gluten-free* • *soy-free* • *no oil added*

1 cup (140 g) cashews

2 tablespoons (29 ml) lemon juice

¼ to ½ cup (60-120 ml) water, as needed

Soak the cashews for a few hours to overnight, or cook in enough water to cover for about 15 minutes over medium heat.

Drain water. Add cashews to a blender with the lemon juice and just enough water to keep the blades working. You will need to scrape down the sides several times and blend. Do this until it's smooth. Store in the refrigerator for about 7 days.

Per ⅛ cup (15 ml) serving: Calories 90, protein 2.5 g, total fat 7.0 g, carbohydrates 4.0 g, sodium 0 mg, fiber 1.0 g

TOFU SOUR CREAM

• gluten-free • no oil added

1 (13.5 oz [350 g]) box silken tofu

2 tablespoons (29 ml) lemon juice

1 to 3 tablespoons (15-44 ml) water, as needed

Add the tofu, lemon juice and 1 tablespoon (15 ml) of water to a blender and blend till smooth. Add more water if needed. You will need to scrape down the sides several times and blend. Do this until it's smooth. Store in the refrigerator for about 7 days.

Per ⅛ cup (15 ml) serving: Calories 24.1, protein 2.1 g, total fat 1.2 g, carbohydrates 1.3 g, sodium 2.2 mg, fiber 0.0 g

TIP: I like to mix this with refried beans in my burritos. Take 1 (15-ounce [439 g]) can of black beans, drained and rinsed, and mix in 1 cup (241 g) cooked, puréed sweet potato with ½ cup (118 ml) salsa, ¼ cup (60 ml) water and ½ teaspoon smoked salt. Mash well, heat and enjoy!

ALMOND RICOTTA

• gluten-free   • soy-free   • no oil added

This ricotta is much richer than Cauliflower Ricotta (recipe on page 34) and is great to serve to non-vegans because it looks so much like the real thing. My friends are always surprised that it's made of almonds. You do have to soak the almonds ahead of time, but if you're in a real pinch you could simmer the almonds and water on the stove for 15 to 20 minutes to soften them a bit on the fly.

MAKES ALMOST 2 CUPS (500 G)

1½ cups (162 g) skinless slivered almonds (or use whole and remove skins after soaking)

1½ cups (355 ml) water

3 tablespoons (45 ml) lemon juice

1 teaspoon salt (optional)

¼ to ½ cup (59-118 ml) water, enough to pull the mixture together

EXTRAS

2 to 3 tablespoons (10-15 g) nutritional yeast

½ cup (10 g) minced fresh basil (or about 1 tablespoon [1.6 g] dried)

1 tablespoon (6 g) minced fresh lemon balm (or 1 teaspoon lemon zest)

Soak the almonds in 1½ cups (355 ml) water for 8 to 24 hours. Drain and add to blender with lemon juice and salt.

Break up the almonds as much as you can, then add water 2 tablespoons (30 ml) at a time until the mixture blends easily. The end product will not be smooth like nut butter, but will look like ricotta.

Per ⅛ cup (31 g) serving: Calories 70.0, protein 0.4 g, total fat 0.0 g, carbohydrates 0.3 g, sodium 145.3 mg, fiber 0.1 g

TIP: This is great with about ½ cup (10 g) fresh oregano blended in. Use anywhere you'd use ricotta.

CARROT CASHEW CHEZ

• *gluten-free*   • *soy-free*   • *no oil added*

Ever wish there were a creamy cheese substitute that didn't cost a fortune, and you could freeze the leftovers for later? I did, and that's why I made up this easy recipe from staples you probably always have— carrots and cashews. Spread the mixture on crackers for a lazy wine-and-cheese dinner or cook with it. It's a must-have ingredient in the Creamy Mexi Mac (page 97). I promise you won't be disappointed.

MAKES ABOUT 2½ CUPS (603 G)

1½ cups (194 g) cashews

1½ cups (192 g) chopped carrots

1½ cups (355 ml) water

¼ cup (59 ml) unsweetened nondairy milk

2 tablespoons (10 g) nutritional yeast

½ teaspoon garlic powder

½ teaspoon onion powder

½ teaspoon salt

Add the cashews, carrots and water to a saucepan. Bring to a boil, then turn heat to medium and simmer for 15 to 20 minutes, until the carrots are soft.

Add the cooked mixture and the rest of the ingredients to a blender and blend until smooth. You will need to stop a few times and scrape the mixture from the sides. If you're having trouble getting it smooth, add more nondairy milk, a tablespoon (15 ml) at a time.

Per ¼ cup (60 g) serving: Calories 120.3, protein 4.3 g, total fat 8.4 g, carbohydrates 8.5 g, sodium 18.5 mg, fiber 1.4 g

SPICED PUMPKIN-CASHEW CREAM CHEZ

•*gluten-free*   •*soy-free*   •*no oil added*

When fall comes around, it brings pumpkin mania with it. I get a little jealous of all the new non-vegan pumpkin goodies, so I get creative and make a few copycats. This recipe is my answer to those pumpkin spice cream cheeses that pop up at every bagel place. It's amazing on a vegan whole grain or cranberry bagel and would work well as a whoopie pie filling, too!

MAKES ABOUT 2 CUPS (482 G)

1 cup (137 g) cashews

1 cup (237 ml) water

¾ cup (184 g) pumpkin purée
(can substitute sweet potato or
butternut squash purée)

2 tablespoons (30 ml) maple syrup

1 tablespoon (15 ml) lemon juice

1 teaspoon cinnamon

½ teaspoon dried ginger

½ teaspoon salt

⅛ teaspoon ground cloves

Soak the cashews in the water for 4 to 24 hours in the refrigerator. Note: If you have a high-speed blender you can soak them more briefly; but if you have a normal blender, soak overnight for best results.

Drain the soaked cashews into a measuring cup and combine them in the blender with the pumpkin, maple syrup, lemon juice, cinnamon, ginger, salt and cloves.

Blend until smooth. You will have to stop and scrape down the sides. It helps if you use a slow speed first to begin to break up the cashews before moving up to the more intense speeds.

If you have a blender that's not very powerful and you need more liquid, add a tablespoon or two (15-30 ml) of the soaking water.

Store in the refrigerator however much you will use in a week.

Per ¼ cup (60 g) serving: Calories 114.8, protein 3.4 g, total fat 7.4 g, carbohydrates 10.6 g, sodium 148.4 mg, fiber 1.5 g

TIP: Make a savory variation by trading mashed avocado for the pumpkin purée and using your favorite savory herbs. You will want to increase the lemon juice to 1½ tablespoons (22 ml) to keep it from browning.

DIY CAJUN SEASONING BLEND

•gluten-free •soy-free •no oil added

If you're looking for a salt-free version or you just can't easily find Cajun seasoning in your area, this little recipe will keep you in spicy goodness for a while. The best part is you can make it as spicy or as mild as you like!

MAKES 3 TABLESPOONS (45 G)

2 teaspoons (10 g) paprika

2 teaspoons (10 g) thyme

2 teaspoons (10 g) oregano or marjoram

1 teaspoon garlic powder

½ teaspoon onion powder

½ to 2 teaspoons cayenne pepper (depending on heat preference)

¼ teaspoon black pepper

¼ teaspoon allspice

⅛ teaspoon cloves

Mix all the ingredients well and store in a lidded container. You can also use a spice grinder or coffee grinder to make it more like store-bought and to distribute the spices more evenly.

SLOW COOKER DRIED BEANS (WITH STOVE-TOP OPTION)

It always surprises me how nervous people get about cooking dry beans. Dried beans are so much cheaper than canned beans! A can of organic dried beans costs about four times what it would cost for you to cook them yourself. Unlike canned beans, home-cooked beans contain no BPA and only the salt you put into them. Plus, you can cook heirloom beans that you can't buy in cans.

ABOUT 6½ CUPS (1.3 KG)

1 pound (0.45 kg) dried beans (such as pintos, navy, chickpeas, black or small red beans)

Water, to cover

TIP: Kidney beans contain the toxin phytohaemagglutinin, which can make you sick. These beans need to get up to a high temperature for at least 10 minutes so it can break down. If you would like to slow cook kidney beans, boil them first for 10 minutes on the stove, and then do the slow cooker method. I usually cook them on the stove since they are already in a pan that I'll have to clean up anyway.

SLOW COOKER METHOD (NOT TO BE USED AS IS WITH KIDNEY BEANS)

Be aware that all beans except chickpeas will come out creamier and softer when cooked in the slow cooker. If this is the wrong texture for the dish you're making, try the stove-top method below. Also, I do not soak my dried beans for the slow cooker, though you certainly can. It will speed up the cooking time.

Sort through the beans for small rocks and other things you don't want in them, then rinse them well. Add them to your 4-quart (4-L) slow cooker and cover with water to about 3 inches (7.6 cm) above the beans. Cook on low 6 to 9 hours. (My tester Julie's favorite way to slow cook beans is on high, which has them ready in 3 to 4 hours.)

STOVE-TOP OPTION

Sort through the beans for small rocks and other things you don't want in your beans, then rinse them well.

If you'd like to soak them, leave them covered in water overnight or all day while you are at work. Drain and then cook as below.

Add the cleaned beans to a large pot with a lid and cover with water to about 2 inches (5 cm) above the beans. Bring to a boil, then lower the heat, cover and simmer until they are tender, about 1½ to 2 hours. Soaking will lessen the cooking time, so check soaked beans after about 45 minutes.

TIP 1: Freeze cooked beans measured out to 1½ cups (380 g) to have the equivalent of 1 can of beans for a recipe.

TIP 2: You can cook a smaller amount of beans. I do this in my 1½- to 2-quart (1½-2 L) slow cookers. Add 1 cup (194 g) dried beans to 3 cups (710 ml) water and cook on low for 6 to 9 hours. (Do not use kidney beans without boiling them first—see tip box on kidney beans at left.)

SUPER-FAST ENCHILADA SAUCE

• *gluten-free* • *soy-free* • *no oil added*

It's tricky to find a vegan enchilada sauce and even harder to find one that has no added oil. This recipe is ridiculously easy because you use a can of crushed tomatoes as your base, add some spices and mix or blend until it's smooth. It doesn't get any easier than this!

MAKES ABOUT 3½ CUPS (828 ML)

1 (28 oz [794 g]) can crushed tomatoes

1 to 2 tablespoons (8-16 g) chili powder, to taste

2 teaspoons (10 g) oregano

1 tablespoon (15 ml) agave nectar, optional

1½ teaspoons (7 g) cumin

1 teaspoon ground garlic

Salt, to taste

Mix all the ingredients; use a blender if you want it to be smoother. Use as is wherever enchilada sauce is called for. You can freeze the leftovers.

Per ½ cup (118 ml) serving: Calories 44.9, protein 1.9 g, total fat 0.3 g, carbohydrates 10.6 g, sodium 149.7 mg, fiber 2.2 g

TIP: Of course you'll use this on enchiladas, but don't forget that it's great on beans and grains, too. It can elevate a plain old dinner into something Instagram worthy!

CAULIFLOWER RICOTTA

• *gluten-free* • *soy-free* • *no oil added*

If you've been looking for a nut- and soy-free ricotta, here it is! It does lend a hint of cauliflower flavor to your dish, but that gets covered up in the Almost Effortless Lasagna on page 102 or by any pasta dish that has a red sauce. You may want to use a bit less of this than your normal ricotta substitution the first time you try it. Make sure to use it on pizza, too!

MAKES ABOUT 3 CUPS (688 G)

1 large head cauliflower

3 tablespoons (45 ml) lemon juice

2 tablespoons (30 ml) unsweetened nondairy milk

1 tablespoon (5 g) nutritional yeast

1½ teaspoons (7 g) oregano or basil

1 teaspoon salt (or to taste)

⅛ teaspoon black pepper

Remove the outer leaves of the cauliflower and cut off any blemished areas. Cut into large florets, place in a soup pot and cover with water. Cook for 8 to 10 minutes, until the stems are turning translucent or at least look less bright white than when you started. Drain.

Carefully add the cooked cauliflower to a food processor and pulse until it starts to look like couscous. Add the rest of the ingredients and pulse until mixed well. Do not turn the food processor on and leave it, or you may end up with puréed cauliflower instead of the slightly chunkier mixture that is closer to the appearance of regular ricotta.

Per ¼ cup (57 g) serving: Calories 19.6, protein 1.7 g, total fat 0.1 g, carbohydrates 3.9 g, sodium 2.0 mg, fiber 1.8 g

TIP: Make a double or triple batch when you find cauliflower on sale or happen to have a ton of it. You can freeze the extra for a time when cauliflower is out of season.

MAPLE WALNUT SAUSAGE PATTIES

• gluten-free   • soy-free   • oil-free option*

Weekend breakfasts at my house are often vegan sausage biscuit or biscuits topped with a creamy gravy and vegan sausage crumbles on top. This sausage comes together in a flash. Don't be put off by the long ingredient list—it's 70% spices, and you will have it measured out in no time. If you already have a special sausage blend, you can use that. I like the blends from Savory Spice Shop. Serve this in one of the biscuits in Chapter 8, Straight-Forward Sides.

MAKES 16 SAUSAGE PATTIES

1 cup (92 g) rolled oats (make sure they are labeled gluten-free to make this dish gluten-free!)

1 cup (100 g) walnuts

2 teaspoons (10 g) rubbed sage

1 teaspoon marjoram

½ teaspoon thyme

½ teaspoon coriander

½ teaspoon ginger powder

½ teaspoon granulated garlic

½ teaspoon onion powder

½ teaspoon rosemary

½ teaspoon salt

¼ teaspoon red pepper flakes or cayenne, optional

⅛ teaspoon pepper

2 tablespoons (14 g) ground flaxseed mixed with 4 tablespoons (60 ml) warm water

2 tablespoons (30 ml) maple syrup

2 tablespoons (30 ml) olive oil (*use applesauce)

Add the oats, walnuts and all the spices (all ingredients above the ground flax seed) to a food processor. Pulse them until you've broken up the oats and walnuts into tiny pieces but they're not yet powdery.

Add the flaxseed mixture, maple syrup and olive oil to the mixture and process until it forms a ball.

Form the patties using a scoop or tablespoon measure, then pat flat to make them into patties.

Heat a nonstick skillet over medium heat. Cook the sausage for about 5 minutes on one side, flip and cook until the other side starts to brown.

If you want to freeze some for later, do not cook them now because they will be too dry when you reheat them. Stack with waxed or parchment paper between patties and freeze them in a container that will protect them from getting smashed.

Per patty with oil: Calories 98.0, protein 2.2 g, total fat 7.5 g, carbohydrates 7.0 g, sodium 73.1 mg, fiber 1.4 g

TIP: Save time by making up a big batch of the sausage spices in an old spice container or other tight-lidded container. Then just add about 1½ tablespoons (20 g) of the mixture to the sausage mix.

CHAI-SPICED ALMOND GRANOLA

• gluten-free option* • *soy-free* • *oil-free option***

Homemade granola is so easy to make that I always wonder why it's so expensive to buy in the store. I like to cook this around the holidays because it makes the house smell wonderful. It's a great vegan yogurt topping.

MAKES ABOUT 3 CUPS (270 G)

2 tablespoons (14 g) ground flaxseed mixed with 4 tablespoons (60 ml) warm water

2 cups (184 g) rolled oats (*make sure oats are marked "gluten-free")

¼ cup (60 ml) maple syrup

¼ cup (54.5 g) coconut oil, melted (**replace oil with 1 tablespoon [7 g] ground flaxseed mixed with 2 tablespoons [30 ml] warm water in addition to the amount above)

½ cup (54 g) slivered almonds

2 teaspoons (10 g) cinnamon

1 teaspoon cardamom

½ teaspoon ground ginger

¼ teaspoon allspice

⅛ teaspoon cloves

¼ teaspoon salt

Preheat oven to 350°F (177°C) and either oil a cookie sheet or cut a piece of parchment paper to fit it.

Add all ingredients but the salt to a medium-sized mixing bowl. Mix well, then add salt to taste.

Pour the mixture on the prepared cookie sheet and press thin so that it's in one large flat piece about ⅛ to ¼ inch (3 to 6 mm) thin. Bake for 20 to 25 minutes, until the edges are browned and the middle is no longer wet.

After it's completely cool, store in an airtight container for up to 2 weeks.

Per ½ cup (45 g) serving: Calories 294.8, protein 6.9 g, total fat 16.5 g, carbohydrates 31.9 g, sodium 97.7 mg, fiber 5.0 g

TIP: Use this granola for a quick and easy crumble. Use berries or cut up enough stone fruit, apples and/or pears to fill up your dish. Toss with a little agave nectar or coconut sugar and a pinch of salt. Cover with the granola. Bake at 350°F (177°C) until the fruit is soft.

CHAPTER 2

SOUPS SAVE THE DAY

Soup is a true hero. It's there for you when you only have a few minutes to cook something. It's also just the thing to stretch a few items in the refrigerator into another meal, which is great for your budget. And, of course, it's always with you when you're sick, helping you feel just a little bit better.

A brothy soup can help you recover from a cold, and a creamy soup can make a meal feel decadent. They range from light to hearty, and there's always one to fit into any dining situation.

Soups come together for a quick anytime meal. In this chapter you'll find everything from soups with Indian spices (page 41) to old favorites like creamy broccoli (page 57). You can use the "cauliflower trick" from the broccoli soup for other creamy soups. Puréed cauliflower adds no fat and a creamy thickness plus a nutritional boost.

INDIAN-SPICED RED LENTIL AND VEGGIE SOUP

•*gluten-free* •*soy-free* •*oil-free option**

This soup is a great for a quick and easy dinner or just to soothe a cold. The lovely Indian spices take this soup far beyond the veggie soup of your childhood. It's great for bean haters, because red lentils melt into the broth so your picky eater won't suspect a thing!

SERVES 4

1 to 2 tablespoons (15-30 ml) olive oil (*or sauté in water)

½ cup (80 g) minced onion

3 cloves garlic, minced

½ cup (74.5 g) chopped bell pepper

1 tablespoon (7.5 g) garam masala

2 teaspoons (10 g) cumin

1 teaspoon turmeric

½ teaspoon ground coriander

4 cups (946 ml) water

2 medium carrots, chopped

1 medium sweet potato, chopped

½ cup (65 g) chopped turnip, potato or daikon radish

¾ cup (144 g) dry red lentils

Salt, to taste

STOVE-TOP METHOD

Heat oil over medium heat in a Dutch oven or soup pot and add the onion once it's hot. Sauté until the onions become translucent, about 5 minutes. Add garlic, bell pepper, garam masala, cumin, turmeric and coriander, then sauté 3 minutes more.

Add the water, carrots, sweet potato, turnip and lentils. Bring to a boil, then simmer for 20 to 30 minutes over medium-low heat until the veggies are tender. Before serving, add salt to taste.

SLOW COOKER METHOD

Heat oil over medium heat and add the onion once it's hot. Sauté until the onions become translucent, about 5 minutes. Add the sautéed onions and everything else except for the salt to your 4-quart (4-L) slow cooker and cook on low for 7 to 10 hours. Before serving, add salt to taste and adjust seasonings as needed.

Per serving with oil: Calories 139.8, protein 4.9 g, total fat 3.8 g, carbohydrates 22.9 g, sodium 38.2 mg, fiber 5.7 g

TIP: Use ½ teaspoon onion powder instead of the onion and skip the sauté step to keep your dishes to a minimum and simplify your morning. This is especially helpful if you're using the slow cooker method.

ASIAN CORN CABBAGE SOUP

*gluten-free option** *oil-free option* *soy-free option**

This soup isn't the prettiest, but the taste is bold and delicious. This recipe is my favorite way to use up the extra cabbage from my CSA.

SERVES 4

½ small onion, minced

1 tablespoon (15 ml) olive oil (*or sauté in water)

2 cloves garlic, minced

1½ cups (105 g) minced mushrooms

Pinch of salt

2 to 3 teaspoons (10-15 g) minced ginger

4 cups (356 g) chopped cabbage

2 cups (282 g) corn kernels (frozen or fresh)

4 cups (946 ml) water

1 tablespoon (5 g) nutritional yeast

2 teaspoons (10 ml) vegetable bouillon

1 teaspoon sesame oil

½ to 1 teaspoon sriracha sauce

1 teaspoon light soy sauce (**or use coconut aminos)

STOVE-TOP METHOD

Sauté the onion in oil (*or water) until it's translucent, then add the garlic and cook 1 more minute. Add mushrooms and a pinch of salt. Sauté until the mushrooms have cooked down and released their liquid, about 10 minutes.

Add everything except sesame, sriracha and soy sauce (**or coconut aminos) to the pot and cook until the cabbage is tender, about 15 minutes.

Before serving, add sesame, sriracha and soy sauce (**or coconut aminos). Adjust seasonings if needed.

SLOW COOKER METHOD

To prep the night before, sauté the onion in oil (*or water) until it's translucent, then add the garlic and cook one more minute. Add mushrooms and a pinch of salt. Sauté until the mushrooms have cooked down and released their liquid. Store the cooked mixture with cut cabbage and corn in the refrigerator overnight.

In the morning, add everything except sesame, sriracha and soy sauce (**or coconut aminos) to your 4-quart (4-L) slow cooker. Cook 7 to 9 hours on low.

Before serving, add sesame, sriracha and soy sauce (**or coconut aminos). Adjust seasonings if needed.

Per serving with oil: Calories 156.8, protein 5.5 g, total fat 5.8 g, carbohydrates 22.4 g, sodium 41.8 mg, fiber 4.9 g

TIP: Cheater Slow Cooker Shortcut: Skip the onion sauté and use ½ teaspoon of onion powder instead. Then add the raw mushrooms into the slow cooker for a throw-it-all-in-and-go meal!

AUTUMN HARVEST NOODLE SOUP

• *gluten-free** • *soy-free* • *oil-free option***

This dish is forgiving, so you can switch turnips or potatoes for the rutabagas, parsnips for carrots, and cabbage for the Brussels sprouts. Also, if you have less than 1 cup (128 g) of carrots after you cut them, it's fine. Just make up any difference with another of the veggies.

SERVES 4

2 to 3 tablespoons (30 to 45 ml) olive oil (**or sauté in water)

½ medium onion, minced (about ½ cup [75 g])

2 cloves garlic, minced

2 teaspoons (10 ml) caraway seeds

1 teaspoon cumin seeds

3 cups (210 g) sliced mushrooms

4 cups (946 ml) water, divided

1 medium rutabaga, diced (about 1½ cups [230 g]) or turnip or potato

2 medium carrots, sliced into half-moons (about 1 cup [128 g])

Extra-large or 8 smallish Brussels sprouts, shredded (about 1 cup [340 g])

1 teaspoon dill weed

¾ cup (79 g) small pasta such as macaroni or bow ties (*use gluten-free pasta*)

Salt and pepper, to taste

Vegan sour cream or Cashew Sour Cream (page 22), for serving (optional)

Heat the oil over medium heat and sauté the onion until translucent, about 3 minutes. Add the garlic, caraway and cumin and sauté until the spices are fragrant, about 1 minute.

Add the mushrooms and sauté until they begin to release their juices. Add 2 cups (473 ml) water, rutabaga, carrots, Brussels sprouts and dill. Cover and reduce heat to medium-low. Simmer until the root veggies are tender, about 30 minutes.

Add 2 cups (473 ml) water and the pasta. Simmer until the noodles are tender, about 15 minutes.

Add salt and pepper to taste. Serve with a side of vegan sour cream or Cashew Sour Cream and a sprig of fresh dill if you have it.

Per serving with oil: Calories 175.6, protein 5.5 g, total fat 7.7 g, carbohydrates 23.8 g, sodium 49.6 mg, fiber 5.8 g

CREOLE OKRA CORN SOUP

• *gluten-free* • *soy-free* • *oil-free option**

Cheryl loves corn, and I love making soup because there's something magical about looking in the refrigerator and coming up with a one-bowl meal. This soup is light enough for an appetizer or for eating in the heat of summer. The corn and okra add texture to the fragrant vegetable broth.

MAKES ABOUT 6 SERVINGS

2 tablespoons (30 ml) olive oil
(*or sauté in water)

½ medium onion, minced

½ medium green pepper, minced

3 cloves garlic, minced

3 cups (710 ml) vegetable broth
(or water with 2 veggie bouillon cubes)

1 (16 oz [454 g]) bag frozen sliced okra
(or equivalent weight of fresh okra)

2 cups (11 oz [328 g]) fresh or frozen
corn kernels

1 (28 oz [794 g]) can crushed tomatoes
(fire-roasted or plain)

1½ teaspoons (7 g) smoked paprika (or
plain paprika plus a few drops of
liquid smoke)

1 teaspoon thyme

1 teaspoon oregano

1 teaspoon marjoram

¼ to ½ teaspoon ground cayenne
pepper, to taste

Salt and pepper, to taste

STOVE-TOP METHOD

Heat oil over medium heat and add the onion once it's hot. Sauté until the onion becomes translucent, about 5 minutes.

Add green pepper and garlic, then sauté 3 minutes more. Stir in the broth, okra, corn, tomatoes and all spices except for the salt and pepper.

Simmer for 20 to 30 minutes over medium heat until the corn and okra are tender. Before serving, add salt and pepper to taste.

SLOW COOKER METHOD

Heat oil over medium heat in a sauté pan and add the onion once it's hot. Sauté until the onion becomes translucent, about 5 minutes.

Add the sautéed onions and everything else except the salt and black pepper to your 4-quart (4-L) slow cooker and cook on low for 7 to 10 hours. Before serving, add salt and pepper to taste.

Per serving with oil: Calories 189.6, protein 5.2 g, total fat 6.0 g, carbohydrates 29.4 g, sodium 647.7 mg, fiber 4.6 g

TIP: Not in the mood to sauté onions for the slow cooker? Use ½ teaspoon onion powder in its place for a throw-and-go soup in the morning!

VEGGIE SPLIT PEA SOUP

gluten-free • *soy-free* • *oil-free option**

It's like clockwork—the leaves start to change colors and I start craving a thick split pea soup. This version adds extra veggies for color and ups the flavor with herbs.

SERVES 4

1 to 2 tablespoons (15-30 ml) olive oil (*or sauté in water)

1 cup (160 g) minced onion

3 cloves garlic, minced

1 cup (133 g) sweet potato chunks

1 cup (89 g) chopped red cabbage

1 cup (128 g) chopped carrots

1 cup (156 g) potato chunks

5 cups (1183 ml) water

1½ cups (296 g) split peas

2 vegetable bouillon cubes

2 bay leaves

2 teaspoons (10 g) thyme

1 teaspoon marjoram

½ teaspoon rosemary

½ teaspoon liquid smoke

Salt and pepper, to taste

STOVE-TOP METHOD

Heat oil over medium heat in a Dutch oven or soup pot and add the onion once it's hot. Sauté until the onions become translucent, about 5 minutes. Add garlic, sweet potato, cabbage, carrots and potato and sauté for 3 to 5 minutes more.

Add the water, split peas, bouillon, bay leaves, thyme, marjoram, rosemary and liquid smoke. Bring to a boil, then simmer for 30 to 45 minutes over medium-low heat until the veggies are tender. Before serving, add salt and pepper to taste.

SLOW COOKER METHOD

Heat oil over medium heat and add the onion once it's hot. Sauté until the onions become translucent, about 5 minutes. Add the sautéed onions and everything else except for salt and pepper to your 4-quart (4-L) slow cooker and cook on low for 7 to 10 hours. Before serving, add salt and pepper to taste and adjust seasonings as needed.

Per serving with oil: Calories 250.6, protein 8.1 g, total fat 3.9 g, carbohydrates 34.9 g, sodium 40.5 mg, fiber 9.5 g

TIP: Not in the mood to sauté onions for the slow cooker? Use ½ teaspoon onion powder in its place for a throw-and-go soup in the morning!

CAULIFLOWER AND RICE SOUP

• *gluten-free*   • *soy-free*   • *oil-free option**

This is my vegan variation on a traditional get-well chicken soup. The cauliflower gives you some texture, and the broth and rice soothe you when your tummy needs a break. You can use cooked noodles in place of the rice if you'd like. It's a great soup to make at the end of a long workweek, too.

SERVES 4

1 to 2 tablespoons (15-30 ml) olive oil
(*or sauté in water)

1 cup (160 g) minced onion

4 cloves garlic, minced

1 cup (128 g) diced carrots

1 cup (101 g) diced celery

2 cups (200 g) small cauliflower florets

4 cups (946 ml) water

1 vegetable bouillon cube
(vegan chickenless flavor if possible)

1 bay leaf

1 tablespoon (2.4 g) thyme

2 teaspoons (10 g) oregano

¼ cup (20 g) nutritional yeast

Salt and pepper, to taste

2 cups (390 g) cooked brown rice,
for serving

STOVE-TOP METHOD

Heat oil over medium heat in a Dutch oven or soup pot and add the onion once it's hot. Sauté until translucent, about 5 minutes. Add garlic and sauté 2 minutes more.

Add the carrots, celery, cauliflower, water, bouillon, bay leaf, thyme and oregano. Bring almost to a boil, then turn down and simmer for 30 to 40 minutes over medium-low heat until the veggies are tender. Once done, stir in the nutritional yeast, then add salt and pepper to taste. Add a scoop of cooked rice to each bowl before serving.

SLOW COOKER METHOD

Heat oil over medium heat and add the onion once it's hot. Sauté until translucent, about 5 minutes. Add the sautéed onions and everything else to your 4-quart (4-L) slow cooker except for the salt, pepper and rice. Cook on low for 7 to 10 hours. Before serving, add salt and pepper to taste and adjust seasonings as needed. Add a scoop of cooked rice to each bowl before serving.

Per serving with oil: Calories 218.9, protein 7.4 g, total fat 4.7 g, carbohydrates 35.7 g, sodium 65.8 mg, fiber 6.2 g

VEGETABLE CHOWDER

• gluten-free • soy-free • oil-free option*

This creamy soup is full of colorful veggies, making it a happy way to brighten up your mood even on the darkest winter day. As a bonus, it's hearty from the potatoes, cauliflower and corn, so this is a great fix for a healthy appetite, too.

SERVES 4

2 tablespoons (30 ml) olive oil
(*or sauté in water)

¼ cup (40 g) minced onion

3 cloves garlic, minced

½ cup (74.5 g) minced bell pepper

1 cup (128 g) chopped carrot

4 cups (946 ml) water

1 cup (240 ml) nondairy milk

2 cups (300 g) potato chunks

1 head cauliflower (1,377 g) broken into florets

1 cup (164 g) corn kernels

1 vegetable bouillon cube

2 bay leaves

1 teaspoon marjoram

1 teaspoon thyme

½ teaspoon smoked or plain paprika

1 cup (156 g) chopped green beans

Salt and pepper, to taste

Cashew Sour Cream (page 22), for serving (optional)

Minced scallions of parsley, for serving (optional)

Heat the oil over medium heat in a Dutch oven or soup pot. Add the onion and sauté for about 5 minutes or until translucent. Add the garlic, bell pepper and carrot and sauté another 3 minutes.

Add the water, milk, potato, cauliflower, corn, bouillon, bay leaves, marjoram, thyme and paprika. Turn the heat to high until it almost boils, then turn it down to medium-low and simmer, covered, for 15 minutes.

Add the green beans and cook until they are tender and the potatoes can be easily pierced with a fork, about 10 minutes.

Before serving, remove 2 to 3 cups (475-700 ml) of the soup, trying to get as much of the potatoes and cauliflower as possible. Add to a blender and blend smooth, then stir back into the soup. Or, if you don't mind a more puréed soup, use an immersion blender.

Lastly, add salt and pepper to taste. Try serving with a dollop of Cashew Sour Cream and minced scallions or parsley to dress it up a little.

Per serving with oil: Calories 200.8, protein 6.7 g, total fat 4.9 g, carbohydrates 35.6 g, sodium 130.2 mg, fiber 8.9 g

BROTHY RAMEN FOR TWO

• gluten-free option* • soy-free option** • oil-free option***

I always have some vegan ramen tucked away for no-brainer dinners. One night I decided to make my own broth and add veggies, and my world changed. This is just as warming as ramen made with store-bought broth, plus it's more nutritious and you can vary the veggies with the season. You can buy plain ramen noodles at an Asian grocery or in bulk online.

SERVES 2

1 to 2 tablespoons (15-30 ml) olive or sunflower oil (***or sauté in water)

¼ cup (40 g) minced onion

2 cloves garlic, minced

½ cup (35 g) sliced mushrooms (or 1 tablespoon [15 g] mushroom powder or 2 tablespoons [30 g] minced dried mushrooms)

¼ cup (37 g) chopped red bell pepper

4½ cups (1 L) water

¼ cup (29 g) chopped daikon, turnip, radish or extra bell pepper

1½ cups (165 g) shredded carrots

1 teaspoon grated ginger, optional

1 vegetable bouillon cube

1 tablespoon (15 ml) soy sauce (**use coconut aminos)

2 single-serving blocks of ramen noodles (*use rice noodles)

2 tablespoons (34 g) miso (I prefer yellow) (**use chickpea miso)

1 tablespoon (5 g) nutritional yeast

OPTIONAL QUICK-COOKING VEGGIES AND EXTRAS

¼ cup (40 g) sliced snow peas

¼ cup (42 g) green peas

½ cup (34 g) minced kale or collards

2 tablespoons (12 g) scallions

1 cup (252 g) cubed tofu

Heat oil in a Dutch oven or soup pot over medium heat. Add the onion and sauté for about 5 minutes or until translucent. Add the garlic, mushrooms and bell pepper and sauté another 5 minutes.

Add the water, daikon, carrots, ginger if using, bouillon cube and soy sauce. Turn heat to high and bring to a boil. Once it's boiling, add the noodles, turn to medium-low heat and cook for 4 to 5 minutes or as the package directs.

Once the noodles are done, stir in the miso, nutritional yeast and any of the optional quick-cooking veggies you'd like to use.

Serve steaming hot with a spoon and chopsticks or a fork.

Per serving with oil: Calories 544.8, protein 14.5 g, total fat 21.1 g, carbohydrates 68.2 g, sodium 2132.6 mg, fiber 6.0 g

SUPER-QUICK CREAMY BROCCOLI SOUP

gluten-free • *soy-free* • *no oil added*

I can still remember the first time I had cream of broccoli soup. It was decadent, creamy and full of delicate spices. This soup has all the flavor of my first bowl and none of the fat. Even better, you can make this any time super-quick if you have some frozen broccoli and California mix.

MAKES 2 LARGE SERVINGS

1½ cups (355 ml) unsweetened nondairy milk

1 cup (240 ml) broth

1 teaspoon thyme

½ to 1 teaspoon garlic powder or 2 to 3 cloves fresh garlic, minced

½ teaspoon marjoram

¼ teaspoon salt

⅛ teaspoon nutmeg

⅛ teaspoon black pepper

1 (12 oz [340 g]) bag of California mix (or about 4 cups [920 g] of fresh mixed cauliflower, broccoli and carrots)

1 cup (91 g) fresh or frozen broccoli

Combine the milk, broth, thyme, garlic, marjoram, salt, nutmeg and black pepper in a medium pan and mix well. Stir in the veggies.

Bring the mixture almost to a boil, then turn down to medium-low heat and simmer until the veggies are tender. This should take about 15 minutes.

Purée with an immersion blender or in a regular blender. Taste and reseason as needed.

Per serving: Calories 108.7, protein 5.0 g, total fat 2.8 g, carbohydrates 17.2 g, sodium 678.6 mg, fiber 6.2 g

WARMING LENTIL SOUP

•*gluten-free* •*soy-free* •*oil-free option**

It's easy to tell that I love my legumes. This lentil soup is especially nice because it's full of veggies and has a Moroccan spice aroma that you can breathe in. It relaxes me right into my weekend. Serve with a big piece of crusty bread.

SERVES 4

1 to 2 tablespoons (15-30ml) of olive oil (*or sauté in water)

½ cup (80 g) chopped onion

3 cloves garlic, minced

½ cup (50.5 g) chopped celery (or ½ teaspoon celery seeds)

1 cup (133 g) chopped sweet potato or butternut squash

1 cup (128 g) chopped carrot

2 cups (475 ml) broth (or water with 1 bouillon cube)

2 cups (475 ml) water

1 (14.5 oz [411 g]) can diced tomatoes (or 1½ cups [241 g] fresh)

1 cup (198 g) brown lentils

3 teaspoons (15 g) marjoram

1½ teaspoons (7 g) cumin

1½ teaspoons (7 g) coriander

1½ teaspoons (7 g) powdered ginger

Salt and black pepper, to taste

STOVE-TOP METHOD

Heat the oil in a soup pot over medium heat. Add the onion and sauté for about 5 minutes or until translucent. Add the garlic and sauté another minute or two.

Add the rest of the ingredients except for the salt and pepper, turn to high heat and bring to a boil.

Cover, turn the heat to low and simmer until the lentils are tender, about 1 hour. Add salt and pepper before serving.

SLOW COOKER METHOD

Heat the oil in a soup pot over medium heat. Add the onion and sauté for about 5 minutes or until translucent. Add the onion and everything else to your 4-quart (4-L) slow cooker. Cook on low for 7 to 10 hours. Before serving, taste and adjust seasonings as needed.

Per serving with oil: Calories 187.5, protein 10.1 g, total fat 3.6 g, carbohydrates 39.1 g, sodium 635.4 mg, fiber 12.3 g

TIP: If you cook in your slow cooker often, it's a great timesaver to have some sautéed onions ready to go. I like to precook a few onions at a time and freeze them in ice-cube trays. Once they're frozen, transfer them to a freezer bag. Use a few cubes instead of sautéing!

CHAPTER 3

SIMPLE STEWS

Stews come together quickly and make flavorful one-bowl meals. I set my rice cooker so that my rice or quinoa is ready when I come home. You can do the same thing in the slow cooker and cook some polenta while you're at work.

You'll find curries (page 70), red beans and rice (page 69), beanless chili (page 65), black beans done up Cuban style (page 63) and a Chinese mapo tofu (page 74).

CUBAN BLACK BEANS OVER COCONUT RICE

• gluten-free   • soy-free   • oil-free option*

One thing I always have in my pantry and freezer is cooked beans. It's so easy to turn them into a quick meal. Here, black beans are lightly seasoned with cumin and are full of cilantro, onion and bell pepper flavor. They go great over the rich coconut rice. In this recipe, you get to skip all the chopping! Instead, you mince everything together in your food processor.

SERVES 4

1 medium red bell pepper, chopped large

½ cup (80 g) chopped onion

¼ cup (4 g) cilantro

3 cloves garlic

1 teaspoon chopped jalapeño pepper (optional)

1 tablespoon (15 ml) olive oil (*or sauté in water)

2 (15 oz [425 g]) cans black beans, rinsed and drained; or 3 cups (720 g) cooked

1 teaspoon cumin

1 teaspoon oregano

½ teaspoon salt

¼ teaspoon black pepper

Coconut Rice (page 64), for serving

Lime wedges, for serving

Add the red bell pepper, onion, cilantro, garlic and jalapeño to a small food processor and process until minced small. (You can chop by hand if you'd prefer.)

Heat the olive oil over medium heat and add the minced veggie mixture. Sauté for a minute or two until the mixture softens. Add the black beans, cumin, oregano, salt and pepper, then cook until heated through, about 10 minutes.

Serve over coconut rice with lime wedges.

Per serving with oil: Calories 212.0, protein 12.1 g, total fat 4.2 g, carbohydrates 34.9 g, sodium 15.3 mg, fiber 12.3 g

COCONUT RICE

• gluten-free • soy-free • no oil added

MAKES ABOUT 2 CUPS (321 G)

1 cup (185 g) long-grain brown rice

1 (14 oz [400 ml]) can light coconut milk

1½ cups (340 ml) vegetable broth

¼ teaspoon salt

¼ teaspoon pepper

Add all the ingredients to a saucepan with a tight-fitting lid. Bring to a boil, then lower heat and simmer until all the liquid is absorbed and the rice is tender, about 30 to 40 minutes.

Per 1 cup (160 g) serving: Calories 259.5, protein 4.0 g, total fat 12.9 g, carbohydrates 31.6 g, sodium 709.9 mg, fiber 1.8 g

"VEGGED-OUT" CHILI

*• gluten-free   • soy-free   • oil-free option**

The minced eggplant and mushrooms take the place of traditional beans and meat. Use leftovers to make burritos or nachos or to add to your morning tofu scramble.

SERVES 4

2 tablespoons (30 ml) olive oil (*or sauté in water)

½ cup (80 g) minced onion

3 cloves garlic, minced

1½ teaspoons ground cumin

1 teaspoon chili powder

½ teaspoon ancho chili powder (or chipotle if you like it hot)

½ teaspoon smoked paprika (or regular paprika plus ¼ teaspoon liquid smoke)

1 (14.5 oz [411 g]) can diced tomatoes

1 cup (82 g) minced eggplant

1 cup (132 g) minced tomatillos

1 cup (164 g) corn kernels

¾ cup (178 ml) porter or stout beer

½ cup (35 g) minced mushrooms

¼ cup (67.5 g) pumpkin or sweet potato purée

1 teaspoon green chilies or jalapeños, minced

½ teaspoon salt

Juice of 1 lime

Cashew Sour Cream (page 22), for serving (optional)

Heat the oil over medium-high heat in a 4 quart (4-L) Dutch oven or soup pot. Once hot, add the onions and sauté until translucent, about 5 minutes. Add the garlic, cumin, chili powders and paprika.

Stir well and cook until the spices release their oils and become fragrant, about 3 minutes.

Add the rest of the ingredients, except for the lime juice. Turn heat to medium-low and cover. Simmer until the veggies are soft and cooked through, about 20 minutes.

Before serving, stir in lime juice. Serve topped with Cashew Sour Cream or tucked into a burrito.

Per serving with oil: Calories 171.9, protein 3.6 g, total fat 8.0 g, carbohydrates 18.8 g, sodium 20.1 mg, fiber 4.2 g

TIP: Not all beer is vegan. You can check to see if the one you are about to buy is on www.barnivore.com

INSIDE-OUT STUFFED PEPPER STEW

*• gluten-free   • oil-free option**

I love stuffed peppers, but I hate the way Cheryl, my picky eater, eats only the insides and leaves the beautiful peppers to go into the compost bin. With this stew, however, she asks for more peppers, and she eats them all! The tempeh makes this stew very protein-rich; and the mushrooms, tomatoes and Italian herbs give it the flavors you remember from childhood.

SERVES 4

1 to 2 tablespoons (15-30 ml) olive oil (*or sauté in water)

½ cup (80 g) minced onion

2 cloves garlic

2 cups (140 g) chopped mushrooms

2 cups (298 g) chopped bell peppers (assorted colors are pretty)

1 (8 oz [227 g]) package of plain soy tempeh, cut in cubes and steamed for 5 minutes

1 (14.5 oz [411 g]) can diced tomatoes (or 1½ cups [241 g] fresh)

1 teaspoon basil

1 teaspoon oregano

1 vegan bouillon cube (mushroom or vegan beefy flavor if possible)

1 teaspoon salt, or to taste

¼ teaspoon black pepper

Heat the oil in a Dutch oven over medium heat. Add the onion and sauté for about 5 minutes, or until translucent.

Add the garlic, mushrooms, bell peppers and tempeh, then sauté for 3 to 5 minutes or until the mushrooms start releasing their liquid.

Stir in the tomatoes, basil, oregano, bouillon, salt and pepper then simmer for 30 minutes so the flavors can meld. Serve over cooked brown rice or quinoa.

Per serving with oil: Calories 205.6, protein 13.6 g, total fat 7.9 g, carbohydrates 19.0 g, sodium 14.7 mg, fiber 2.4 g

TIP: Make a soy-free version by using a variation on the Cauliflower Mexi Mince (page 18). Instead of the Mexican spices, use an Italian seasoning blend or a mix of basil, oregano and rosemary. You could also use cooked, leftover bulgur in place of the tempeh.

VEGGIE-FUL RICE AND BEANS

• gluten-free   • soy-free   • oil-free option*

These rice and beans are fortified with carrots and sweet potatoes, making a traditional favorite even better and ever so slightly sweeter. I like to make mine mild and serve hot sauce on the side, but you can make yours fiery and serve it spicy instead!

SERVES 4

2 tablespoons (30 ml) olive oil (*or sauté in water)

½ small onion, minced

3 cloves garlic, minced

1 cup (149 g) green bell pepper, minced

1 medium carrot, minced or shredded

4 cups (946 ml) water

1½ cups (295 g) dried small red beans

1 cup (133 g) diced sweet potato

2 teaspoons (10 g) Cajun seasoning, no salt added

½ to 1 teaspoon cayenne pepper (optional)

A few dashes liquid smoke

Salt and pepper, to taste

Cooked long-grain brown rice, for serving

Hot pepper sauce such as Tabasco, for serving

STOVE-TOP METHOD

Heat the oil over medium-high heat in a 4-quart (4-L) Dutch oven or soup pot. When hot, add onions and sauté until translucent, about 5 minutes. Then add the garlic, green bell pepper and carrot. Sauté until the green pepper begins to get tender, about 5 minutes.

Add the water, beans, sweet potato, Cajun seasoning, cayenne pepper (if you're using it) and liquid smoke. Bring to a boil, then cover and simmer on low about 1 to 2 hours. The beans should be soft and the sweet potato should have dissolved into the mix.

Taste and add more Cajun seasoning if needed, then add salt and pepper to taste. Serve over cooked rice or your favorite cooked grain with hot sauce on the side.

SLOW COOKER METHOD

Please note that if you use kidney beans, they have a toxin called phytohaemagglutinin that can make you sick. To break it down, cook them at a high temperature for at least 10 minutes. Boil them for 10 minutes before proceeding with the slow cooker.

Add all the ingredients except for salt and pepper to a 4-quart (4-L) slow cooker. Cook on low for 8 to 10 hours.

Taste and add more Cajun seasoning if needed, then add salt and pepper to taste. Serve over cooked rice or your favorite cooked grain with hot sauce on the side.

Per serving with oil: Calories 243.5, protein 16.0 g, total fat 7.0 g, carbohydrates 59.7g, sodium 68.8 mg, fiber 35.7 g

TIP: Small red beans are labeled just that, but you can use any small red bean. If you use a different bean, the recipe could take a little longer to cook on the stove.

INDIAN-STYLE POTATO AND PEAS (ALOO MUTTER)

• gluten-free   • soy-free   • oil-free option*

This stew boasts potatoes, peas and a blend of spices that come together for a great Indian dinner. It pairs perfectly with steamed brown basmati rice and the Cauliflower Masala on page 73.

SERVES 4

2 tablespoons (30 ml) olive oil (*use nonstick pan)

1 tablespoon (6 g) cumin seeds

1½ teaspoons (7 g) garam masala

¼ cup (40 g) minced onion

1 tablespoon (8 g) minced fresh ginger

2 cloves garlic, minced

1 teaspoon turmeric

¼ to ½ teaspoon chili powder

4 cups potato chunks (about 24 oz [680 g])

1½ cups (355 ml) water

2 cups (290 g) peas

1 cup (250 g) crushed tomatoes

Salt, to taste

Heat the oil in a Dutch oven over medium heat. Once it's hot, add the cumin seeds and toast them until fragrant, about 1 minute. Stir in the garam masala and onion. Cook until the onion is translucent, about 3 to 5 minutes.

Add the ginger, garlic, turmeric and chili powder and sauté 2 to 3 minutes more. Then add the potato chunks and water. Bring to a boil.

Once it's boiling, lower heat to medium and cook until the potatoes are tender, about 10 to 15 minutes. The water will boil down some, but do not let it cook all the way dry.

When potatoes are tender, add the peas and tomatoes. Cover and cook for 10 to 15 minutes more, until the peas are done to your liking.

Before serving, add salt to taste and more garam masala or chili powder if the flavor doesn't pop enough for you.

Per serving with oil: Calories 249.2, protein 7.7 g, total fat 7.3 g, carbohydrates 40.3 g, sodium 110.7 mg, fiber 8.7 g

CAULIFLOWER MASALA

• *gluten-free* • *soy-free* • *oil-free option**

Masala is many people's introduction to Indian food. It's my picky eater's favorite, so I take full advantage to get yet more veggies in her. Cauliflower is perfect in this dish because it stands up to the flavorful sauce and does not get mushy. This dish is not spicy at all, so it's perfect for kids and picky eaters of all ages.

SERVES 4

2 tablespoons (30 ml) olive oil (*use nonstick pan or sauté in water)

¼ cup (40 g) minced onion

2 teaspoons (10 g) garam masala

1 teaspoon ground coriander

1 teaspoon ground cumin

½ teaspoon turmeric

3 teaspoons (6 g) grated fresh ginger

1 garlic clove, minced

1 (14.4 oz [411 g]) can of crushed tomatoes (or 1½ cups [241 g])

1 cup (237 ml) vegetable broth (or 1 cup water [237 ml] plus ½ veggie bouillon cube)

½ small head of cauliflower, broken into florets (or 1 [12 oz/340 g] bag of frozen cauliflower florets)

½ cup (120 ml) unsweetened nondairy milk

Salt, to taste

Heat the oil in a Dutch oven over medium heat. Add the onion and sauté for about 5 minutes or until translucent.

Add the garam masala, coriander, cumin and turmeric. Cook until the spices become fragrant, about 1 to 2 minutes. Then add the ginger and garlic and sauté 1 to 2 minutes.

Add the tomatoes, broth and cauliflower florets and bring to a boil.

Once it's boiling, lower heat to medium and cook until the cauliflower is tender, about 10 minutes.

Before serving, add the nondairy milk and salt to taste.

Per serving with oil: Calories 97.0, protein 1.5 g, total fat 7.5 g, carbohydrates 7.2 g, sodium 274.1 mg, fiber 1.9 g

TIP: Make this rich and thick by using full-fat coconut milk in place of the nondairy milk, or stir in about ¼ cup (60 ml) Cashew Sour Cream (page 22).

MAPO TOFU

• gluten-free option* • no oil added

This is the easiest Chinese dish to throw together when you're just too tired to cook. Since it's a stew instead of a stir-fry, you don't have to concentrate the entire time. It's full of flavor, with ginger, mushrooms and tofu in a spicy red sauce.

SERVES 4

1 (8 oz [349 g]) package of mushrooms, chopped (about 3 cups [177 g])

3 cloves garlic, minced

1 cup (235 ml) water or broth

3 tablespoons (49 g) tomato paste

1 heaping tablespoon (8 g) grated fresh ginger

2 tablespoons (30 ml) soy sauce (*use gluten-free)

1 tablespoon (15 ml) rice wine vinegar

1 tablespoon (15 ml) agave nectar

½ to 1 tablespoon (7–15 ml) sriracha, to taste

1 (12.3 oz [349 g]) package of firm silken tofu, cut into cubes

1 cup (160 g) peas or chopped broccoli

Steamed brown rice, for serving

Add the mushrooms and garlic to a large saucepan and dry sauté over medium heat until the mushrooms cook down, 5 to 10 minutes.

Stir in the water or broth, tomato paste, ginger, soy sauce, vinegar, agave nectar and sriracha. Bring almost to a boil, then add the tofu and peas or broccoli and lower the heat to medium-low.

Cook until the veggies are tender, about 10 minutes, and serve over steamed brown rice.

Per serving without rice: Calories 106.1, protein 9.9 g, total fat 1.4 g, carbohydrates 16.0 g, sodium 685.9 mg, fiber 3.1 g

TIP: You can make this in a 4-quart (4-L) slow cooker by adding everything but the broccoli or peas, then cooking on low 8 to 9 hours. When you get home, add the veggies and cook another 30 minutes. Taste and adjust seasonings before serving.

POTATO GREEN BEAN STEW

• gluten-free   • soy-free   • oil-free option*

This simple stew has a delicate broth. If you start with a good-quality broth or bouillon as the base, the bay leaf and winter squash will chime in to make your stew one of the best comfort foods you've ever had. You can use white beans if you'd like; they will taste just as good as chickpeas.

SERVES 4

1 to 2 tablespoons (15-30 ml) of olive oil (*or sauté in water)

¼ cup (40 g) chopped onion

2 cloves garlic, minced

2 cups (475 ml) vegetable broth or 2 cups (475 ml) water with 1 bouillon cube

2 cups (280 g) diced winter squash such as butternut or acorn

2 cups (312 g) diced potatoes

1 (15 oz [425 g]) can chickpeas, rinsed and drained, or 1½ cups (300 g) cooked

1 bay leaf

2 cups (220 g) green beans, cut in half

Salt and pepper, to taste

Heat the oil in a soup pot over medium heat. Add the onion and sauté for about 5 minutes or until translucent. Add the garlic and sauté a minute or two more.

Add the broth, squash, potatoes, chickpeas and bay leaf. Turn up to high heat and bring almost to a boil.

Turn down the heat to low and simmer until the potatoes are tender, about 15 minutes. Uncover, stir in the green beans and cook until they are tender. Add salt and pepper. Serve in a bowl and make sure to add some of the broth.

Per serving with oil: Calories 260.3, protein 7.8 g, total fat 4.6 g, carbohydrates 49.7 g, sodium 759.4 mg, fiber 10.8 g

WHITE BEAN KALE STEW

• gluten-free   • soy-free   • oil-free option*

This is an easy stew that is as full of comfort as it is of kale. The carrots add a slight sweetness, and the herbs give it a flavor boost. This is great as is, over polenta or even over a toasted piece of whole grain bread.

. . . .

SERVES 4

. . . .

1 to 2 tablespoons (15-30 ml) olive oil (*or sauté in water)

¼ cup (40 g) minced onion

2 cloves garlic, minced

1 (14.5 oz [438 g]) can diced tomatoes (or 1½ cups [241 g] fresh)

1 (14.5 ounce [425 g]) can cannellini or navy beans, rinsed (or 1½ cups [300 g] cooked)

1 cup (138 g) sliced carrots

1 teaspoon basil

½ teaspoon rosemary

1½ packed cups (100 g) fresh or frozen kale or other green

Salt and pepper, to taste

Heat the oil in a soup pot over medium heat . Add the onion and sauté for about 5 minutes or until translucent. Add the garlic and sauté a minute or two more. Add tomatoes, beans, carrots, basil and rosemary.

Cover, turn the heat to medium-low and simmer until the carrots are tender, about 15 minutes. Uncover, stir in the kale and cook until heated thoroughly. Add salt and pepper, then serve over your favorite grain, polenta, pasta or toast.

. . . .

Per serving with oil: Calories 171.7, protein 7.6 g, total fat 4.3 g, carbohydrates 27.9 g, sodium 38.8 mg, fiber 9.9 g

. . . .

FLASHBACK CHILI

• *gluten-free option** • *soy-free* • *no oil added*

This chili reminds me of one I ate when I first went meatless. The base ingredients came out of a box, and I added beans and tomatoes. Honestly, making mine from scratch is just as easy, and you'll probably have leftovers to use in burritos or to ladle over nachos.

MAKES 8 SERVINGS

3 (15.5 oz [340 g]) cans beans or 4½ cups (770 g) cooked (pinto, black, white or assorted)

1 (28 oz [794 g]) can crushed or diced tomatoes (or 3 cups [482 g] fresh)

½ cup bulgur (*use quinoa, millet or a combination of the two)

2½ cups (541 ml) water

1 to 2 vegetable bouillon cubes, depending on saltiness

2 tablespoons (10 g) nutritional yeast (optional)

1½ teaspoons (7 g) cumin

1½ teaspoons (7 g) chili powder

1 teaspoon garlic powder (or 3 cloves garlic, minced)

1 teaspoon smoked paprika

1 teaspoon ancho or chipotle chili powder

Salt, to taste

TOPPING IDEAS

Chopped cilantro

Avocado cubes

Fresh chopped tomatoes

Fresh chopped onions

Vegan shredded cheese

Cashew Sour Cream (page 22) with a few squeezes of lime juice

Lime wedges

STOVE-TOP METHOD

Add everything except the salt to a large pot or Dutch oven. Bring to a boil, then simmer for 20 to 25 minutes over medium-low heat until the veggies are tender. Before serving, add salt to taste.

SLOW COOKER METHOD

Add everything except salt to your 4-quart (4-L) slow cooker and cook on low for 7 to 10 hours. Before serving, add salt to taste and adjust seasonings as needed.

Per serving without toppings: Calories 191.0, protein 10.5 g, total fat 0.8 g, carbohydrates 35.8 g, sodium 236.3 mg, fiber 11.0 g

TIP: If you have heirloom beans to use up, this is a great recipe for them. You'll just need to remember to cook them ahead of time. This is my favorite way to finish off a few bags that have less than ¼ cup (50 g) in them.

CHAPTER 4

PUSHOVER PASTAS

Pasta is where my family turns if there's no time to make dinner. I've even added in a sauce recipe that you can freeze and use any time.

There are veggie-centric pestos with avocado and cauliflower (pages 86 and 89), one-pot lo mein (page 93) and vodka sauce pastas (page 90). Mexi-Mac (page 97) and Potpie Pasta (page 94) will get dinner on the table quickly and keep the pickiest of eaters interested.

MUSHROOM RED PEPPER PASTA SAUCE

• *gluten-free*   • *soy-free*   • *oil-free option**

Everyone needs a pasta sauce recipe that can be made without a lot of hassle. The rich flavor comes from the mushrooms and a little balsamic vinegar. Use as is on cooked pasta or in the Almost Effortless Lasagna recipe on page 102.

MAKES ABOUT 5 CUPS (1.2 L)

1 to 2 tablespoons (15-30 ml) olive oil (*or sauté in water)

4 cups chopped mushrooms (1 [8 oz/226 g] package)

½ cup (74.5 g) chopped red bell pepper

1 (28 oz [794 g]) can crushed tomatoes (or 3 cups [482 g] fresh)

2 teaspoons (10 ml) balsamic vinegar

1 teaspoon basil

1 teaspoon oregano

½ teaspoon salt, to taste

⅛ teaspoon black pepper

Heat the oil in a soup pot over medium heat. Add the mushrooms and bell pepper and sauté for about 5 minutes.

Add the rest of the ingredients and simmer, covered, for 20 to 30 minutes. Before serving or freezing, you can add any extras you'd enjoy, such as additional herbs, more balsamic vinegar or red wine.

Per 1 cup (237 ml) serving with oil: Calories 93.7, protein 4.5 g, total fat 3.4 g, carbohydrates 14.9 g, sodium 212.6 mg, fiber 4.0 g

TIP: This freezes well. You can use half for one meal the day you make it and save the rest for another day.

EASY AVOCADO LEMON BASIL PESTO

• gluten-free • soy-free • no added oil

Don't let the specialty basil intimidate you. If you don't have lemon basil, you can use regular basil and add lemon zest, extra lemon juice or another lemony herb like lemon verbena or lemon balm. This rich, creamy pasta sauce comes together in minutes and has a bright lemon and herb flavor.

SERVES 3 TO 4, BUT YOU CAN EASILY DOUBLE OR TRIPLE THE RECIPE

1 medium ripe avocado

½ cup (12 g) fresh lemon basil (or substitute regular basil)

1 (2- to 4-inch [5- to 10-cm]) sprig fresh thyme

1 tablespoon (3 g) fresh oregano leaves

1 tablespoon (15 ml) lemon juice

½ teaspoon salt, to taste

Pepper, to taste

¼ cup (59 ml) water plus more if needed

½ lb (227 g) cooked whole-wheat angel-hair pasta

Scoop out the avocado. Put the avocado flesh, lemon basil, leaves from the thyme and oregano, lemon juice, salt and water in a blender and blend well until the herbs are puréed.

If the purée is still too thick, add 2 more tablespoons (30 ml) of water and blend again. Toss with the cooked whole-wheat angel-hair pasta.

Per serving: Calories 94.4, protein 2.1 g, total fat 8.7 g, carbohydrates 5.5 g, sodium 0.2 mg, fiber 5.5 g

> **TIP:** This pesto comes together in minutes, so put your pasta in the boiling water while you make it. The pesto will be ready to toss with your piping hot, perfectly cooked pasta. You'll be out of the kitchen before the pesto has time to get too hot!

CREAMY CAULIFLOWER PESTO PASTA

• gluten-free option* • soy-free • no oil added

This alfredo-like sauce has no added oil and gets an upgrade with fresh basil. The creamy sauce is veggie-based, and there are lots of extra veggies thrown in. Don't be surprised that the sauce becomes light green when you add the basil.

SERVES 4

3½ cups (350 g) fresh cauliflower florets or 1 (12 oz [340 g]) bag frozen florets

1½ cups (355 ml) water

2 vegetable bouillon cubes

3 cups (672 g) dry whole-wheat rotini pasta (*use gluten-free pasta)

2½ cups (320 g) chopped assorted veggies, such as small broccoli florets, carrots, zucchini, Italian flat green beans (or 1 [12 oz/340 g] bag frozen Italian veggie mix)

½ cup (120 g) unsweetened nondairy milk

1 tablespoon (5 g) nutritional yeast

½ cup (12 g) fresh basil leaves

Salt and pepper, to taste

Add the cauliflower, water and bouillon cubes to a pot and bring to a simmer over medium-high heat. Cook until the cauliflower is tender, about 10 minutes.

While waiting for the cauliflower, start heating water for the pasta in a large pot. When the water boils, add the pasta and turn down the heat to medium. Cook your pasta according to package directions, but throw in the veggies about 5 minutes before the pasta is done. Drain.

Carefully add the cauliflower and broth to a blender with the milk, nutritional yeast and basil. Blend until puréed. Then add salt and pepper to taste.

Add the sauce, pasta and veggies back into the large pot and heat over medium-low heat for about 2 to 3 minutes, or until piping hot.

Per serving with broccoli: Calories 219.8, protein 10.6 g, total fat 2.1 g, carbohydrates 40.2 g, sodium 655.6 mg, fiber 8.5 g

ONE-POT VEGGIE VODKA SAUCE PASTA

• *gluten-free option** • *soy-free* • *no added oil*

This has all the ease you expect from a one-pot meal. You cook the pasta right in the creamy tomato sauce, which has the barest hint of vodka and mushrooms, carrots and eggplant.

SERVES 4

2½ cups (8 oz [227 g]) rotini pasta (*use gluten-free pasta)

¾ cup (52.5 g) mushrooms, chopped small

¾ cup (82.5 g) shredded carrots

½ cup (41 g) minced eggplant

2 cups (18 oz [510 g]) vegan marinara sauce or Mushroom Red Pepper Pasta Sauce (page 85)

2 cups (474 ml) plain nondairy milk, unsweetened

1 tablespoon (15 ml) vodka (optional)

2 teaspoons (10 ml) tomato paste

2 teaspoons (3.3 g) nutritional yeast

1 teaspoon basil

½ teaspoon oregano

¼ teaspoon pepper flakes

⅛ teaspoon onion powder

Salt, to taste

Add everything but the salt to a deep skillet and push the pasta underneath the liquid. Bring to a boil, then turn the heat down to medium-low and simmer until the pasta is al dente, about 10 minutes.

Stir every few minutes so everything doesn't stick to the bottom of the pan. Cook for about 9 minutes or until the pasta is tender. The timing will vary depending on the shape and kind of pasta you use. Taste and add salt if needed.

Per serving: Calories 263.0, protein 7.3 g, total fat 6.8 g, carbohydrates 43.4 g, sodium 696.4 mg, fiber 8.5 g

ONE-POT VEGETABLE LO MEIN

• *gluten-free option** • *soy-free option*** • *no oil added*

This is the one-pot dish to make when you're craving Chinese takeout. Noodles with a spicy Asian sauce, veggies and your choice of extras make for an easy dinner after a hard day.

SERVES 6

1 (13.5 oz [374 g]) box whole-wheat spaghetti (*use gluten-free pasta)

2½ cups (592 ml) water

1½ cups (355 ml) vegetable broth (can be vegan chickenless broth)

¼ cup + 1 tablespoon (77 ml) soy sauce (**use coconut aminos)

2 cloves garlic, minced

1 tablespoon (15 ml) rice wine vinegar

1 tablespoon (6 g) grated fresh ginger

1 cup (92 g) julienne bell peppers

1 cup (70 g) diced mushrooms

1 cup (166 g) vegan meatless crumbles, crumbled tempeh or broccoli

1 (8 oz [227 g]) can of diced water chestnuts

Scallions, for serving

Sriracha, for serving

Add everything but the scallions and sriracha to a deep skillet and push the pasta underneath the liquid. Bring to a boil, then turn the heat down to medium-low and simmer until the pasta is al dente, about 10 minutes. You can add a few tablespoons of water if needed during cooking. Serve with scallions and some sriracha.

Per serving less scallions: Calories 354.8, protein 18.8 g, total fat 2.8 g, carbohydrates 63.5 g, sodium 1126.0 mg, fiber 8.2 g

VEGGIE "POTPIE" PASTA

• *gluten-free option** • *soy-free* • *oil-free option***

I love the creamy flavor of a veggie potpie, but I don't always have the time or energy to make one. This pasta comes to the rescue with a quick-to-make white-bean-based creamy sauce studded with veggies.

SERVES 6

3 cups (315 g) whole-wheat pasta shells (*use gluten-free and cook per box directions)

1 (15.5 oz [340 g]) can cannellini beans or 1½ cups (300 g) homemade

2 cups (474 ml) unsweetened nondairy milk

¼ cup (20 g) nutritional yeast

1 teaspoon marjoram

1 teaspoon thyme

½ teaspoon sage

¼ teaspoon rosemary

½ teaspoon salt

¼ teaspoon black pepper

1 to 2 tablespoons (15-30 ml) olive oil (**or sauté in water)

¼ cup (40 g) minced onions

½ cup (35 g) chopped mushrooms

2 cloves garlic, minced

1 (1 lb [454 g]) package frozen veggies (carrots, peas, corn, lima beans or edamame) or about 3½ cups (400 g) fresh

1 (12 oz [340 g]) package frozen broccoli florets or about 3 cups (465 g) fresh

Cook the pasta according to package directions until just al dente, drain and set aside.

While the pasta is cooking, make the sauce by combining the beans, milk, nutritional yeast, marjoram, thyme, sage, rosemary, salt and pepper in a blender and blend until smooth, then set aside.

Heat the oil in a large sauté pan—one that's big enough to hold the veggies and pasta—over medium heat. Add the onion and sauté for about 5 minutes or until translucent. Then stir in the mushrooms and garlic and cook until the mushrooms cook down, about 10 minutes.

Add the mixed veggies and cook about 10 minutes. Then add the sauce and broccoli. Cook until the broccoli and carrots are tender and can be pierced with a fork.

Stir in the pasta and heat for another minute or two, until the pasta is hot.

Per serving with oil and peas: Calories 282.7, protein 14.1 g, total fat 4.3 g, carbohydrates 48.1 g, sodium 211.7 mg, fiber 11.3 g

TIP: If you want a richer, creamier sauce, add up to ½ cup (55 g) cashews to the blender ingredients. Chop them if they are large and they will soften faster, even though you have not soaked them first. Cashew pieces are much less expensive than whole nuts!

CREAMY MEXI MAC

• *gluten-free option** • *soy-free* • *oil-free option***

Warm, gooey pasta dishes that pack a flavor punch are a great way to end a hard day. This one is comfort in a bowl. It uses the Carrot Cashew Chez from page 27, but you can use a premade vegan nacho cheese or even a vegan cheese such as Daiya in its place.

. . . .

SERVES 6

. . . .

1 tablespoon (15 ml) olive oil
(**or sauté in water)

½ cup (80 g) chopped onion

2 cloves garlic, minced

2 cups (298 g) chopped bell pepper

1 can (15 oz [425 g]) black beans rinsed and drained or 1½ cups (258 g) homemade

1 cup (154 g) corn kernels

½ cup (120 g) vegan enchilada sauce

1 cup (165 g) vegan grounds, Cauliflower Mexi Mince (page 18) or store-bought crumbles

1 cup (240 g) Carrot Cashew Chez (page 24), vegan cheese or premade vegan nacho cheese sauce

¼ cup (60 ml) unsweetened nondairy milk

¼ teaspoon salt, or to taste

½ (13.25 oz [375 g]) box macaroni pasta (*use gluten-free), cooked per directions on box

Heat the oil in a large pot over medium-high heat. Once hot, add the onions and sauté until translucent. Add the garlic and bell peppers and sauté for about 5 more minutes until the peppers soften.

Turn down the heat to medium and add all the other ingredients to the pot and mix well. Cook until heated through.

. . . .

Per serving with oil: Calories 494.7, protein 19.6 g, total fat 13.7 g, carbohydrates 79.1 g, sodium 86.4 mg, fiber 11.5 g

. . . .

SINGAPORE MAI FUN (CURRY THIN RICE NOODLES)

• *gluten-free option** • *soy-free option*** • *oil-free option****

Sometimes you need some zing in your Chinese food. The curry powder is the key to this Singapore Mai Fun. Otherwise it would just be plain old mai fun, which refers to the super-skinny rice noodles. They cook al dente, giving a great texture to this slightly spicy curried rice noodle dish.

. . . .

SERVES 4

. . . .

1 (8 oz [227 g]) box mai fun noodles (very thin brown rice noodles if possible)

⅔ cup (157 ml) water

⅓ cup (79 ml) soy sauce (*use gluten-free or **use coconut aminos)

1 tablespoon (15 g) rice wine vinegar

1 tablespoon (6 g) grated ginger

3 cloves garlic, minced

2 teaspoons (10 ml) sesame oil (***leave out or substitute tahini)

2 tablespoons (59 ml) cooking oil

1 medium onion, julienned

2 medium bell peppers, julienned

2 cups (220 g) shredded carrot or broccoli slaw

2 cups (140 g) shredded cabbage (red or green)

1 tablespoon (6 g) curry powder (hot or mild)

Soak the noodles in enough warm water to cover them. You'll need to soak them for 6 to 8 minutes, until they soften but are a little al dente.

In a small bowl, combine the water, soy sauce, rice wine vinegar, ginger, garlic and sesame oil. This is the sauce mixture.

Heat the oil in a large sauté pan or wok over medium-high heat. Once it's hot, add the onions and cook for 2 minutes until they start to soften. Add the bell peppers, carrots and cabbage and sauté about 5 minutes more.

If you aren't sure how hot your curry powder is, start with ½ tablespoon (3 g), then taste and decide whether you want the rest. Sprinkle the curry powder over the veggies, mix well and adjust if necessary. Now add the sauce mixture and the soaked noodles.

The hard part is getting the veggies mixed in well with the noodles. I use tongs for that part. After it's all mixed well, serve.

. . . .

Per serving with oil: Calories 361.5, protein 3.4 g, total fat 10.1 g, carbohydrates 65.4 g, sodium 1495.1 mg, fiber 5.1 g

. . . .

RED CURRY PEANUT NOODLES

• gluten-free option*   • soy-free option**   • oil-free option***

When it's too hot even to consider turning on the stove, this dish is a lifesaver. Tossed with cooked chilled noodles or cucumber, this creamy sauce has hints of ginger, sesame and red curry paste.

SERVES 4

¾ cup (177 ml) water, divided

½ cup (129 g) smooth peanut butter

2 tablespoons (30 ml) soy sauce (*use gluten-free or ***coconut aminos)

1 tablespoon (15 ml) rice wine vinegar

2 teaspoons (10 ml) sesame oil (***leave out or substitute tahini)

2 teaspoons (10 ml) red curry paste

¾ teaspoon ground ginger

4 servings cooked whole-wheat angel-hair pasta, (**cooked rice noodles or **cucumber "pasta") for serving

Whisk all the sauce ingredients together in a mixing bowl except for ¼ cup (60 ml) of the water. If the sauce is thicker than you like, add a few tablespoons of water (up to ¼ cup [60 ml]) until it's thin enough to coat the pasta evenly.

Toss with the cooked noodles and serve room temperature or chilled.

Per serving with oil: Calories 852.0, protein 11.6 g, total fat 67.0 g, carbohydrates 55.0 g, sodium 861.6 mg, fiber 4.0 g

TIP: You can make cucumber noodles without any of those fancy spiral cutters. Just use your peeler to slice super-thin pieces from top to bottom of a peeled cucumber until you reach the seeds. I use one large cucumber per person.

ALMOST EFFORTLESS LASAGNA

• gluten-free option* • soy-free • oil-free option**

If you have the right ingredients on hand, you can whip up a lasagna in minutes. I don't cook my noodles ahead of time; I just let them cook right in the pan with everything else. You can use any veggie from frozen spinach to fresh vegetables from your farmers' market.

SERVES 8

3 cups (710 ml) pasta sauce, Mushroom Red Pepper Pasta Sauce recipe (page 85) or your favorite store-bought sauce

½ (1 pound [454 g]) box of whole-wheat or regular lasagna (*use gluten-free)

3 cups (600 g) vegan ricotta, or Cauliflower Ricotta (page 33) or Almond Ricotta (page 24)

1 (12 oz [340 g]) bag frozen cut leaf spinach (or about 2 pounds [907 g] fresh, sautéed and drained)

½ cup (118 ml) unsweetened nondairy milk

¼ cup (20 g) nutritional yeast

Preheat oven to 350°F (177°C) and prepare two loaf pans by oiling or **lining with parchment paper. I like to use two loaf pans so I can serve one lasagna now and freeze the second for later, but you can cook both at once or use a rectangular baking pan.

The directions below are per loaf pan—repeat for each one.

LAYER THE INGREDIENTS EVENLY IN THE PREPARED LOAF PAN, IN THIS ORDER:

- ½ cup (118 ml) sauce
- uncooked lasagna noodles
- ½ cup (75 g) vegan ricotta of choice
- uncooked lasagna noodles
- ½ cup (118 ml) sauce
- ½ of the spinach
- uncooked lasagna noodles
- ½ cup (75 g) vegan ricotta of choice
- uncooked lasagna noodles
- mix the last ½ cup (118 ml) sauce with ¼ cup (59 ml) unsweetened nondairy milk and 2 tablespoons (10 g) nutritional yeast

Cover with foil and bake for 40 to 55 minutes, until the noodles are cooked through. You can test by seeing if a fork will go easily into the noodles.

If you do freeze one, allow it to thaw in the refrigerator overnight before baking as above.

Per serving: Calories 260.8, protein 13.2 g, total fat 3.6 g, carbohydrates 54.1 g, sodium 109.8 mg, fiber 11.1 g

TIP: Add some crumbled tempeh, vegan meatless crumbles or white beans to the spinach layer to make it heartier.

CHAPTER 5

MANAGEABLE MAINS

All of these recipes pay off once you sit down to dinner. Many cook quickly, while others come together quickly and cook for a longer "hands-off" time in the oven. That's time in which you can do anything you'd rather do than work in the kitchen.

There is Mexican Fried Rice (page 108), Sweet Potato Ropa (page 120), Holiday Stuffing Casserole (page 111) and even Apple Zucchini Buckwheat Pancakes (page 127), because breakfast for dinner is sometimes just what you need.

NO-THINKING VEGGIE QUINOA

• *gluten-free*   • *soy-free*   • *oil-free option**

Quinoa is my favorite quick-cooking grain. This dish is prepared like a casserole, with chickpeas and a mix of veggies and herbs. While it's baking, you can relax with a glass of wine, help your kids with homework or tidy up a bit.

SERVES 4

1 cup (170 g) quinoa, rinsed

1 (15 oz [425 g]) can chickpeas, rinsed and drained or 1½ cups (300 g) cooked

1½ cups (355 ml) vegetable broth (or water with 1 bouillon cube)

1 (12 oz [340 g]) bag frozen veggie Italian mix (or 3 cups [450 g] mixed veggies like zucchini, red bell pepper, carrots, green beans and lima beans)

2 teaspoons (2 g) basil

1 teaspoon oregano

¼ teaspoon salt

⅛ teaspoon black pepper

Preheat oven to 400°F (204°C) and spray an 8.5" x 11" (21 x 28 cm) casserole dish (*leave out the oil, but be prepared to soak the pan before cleaning).

Mix all the ingredients in a large mixing bowl, then pour into the prepared casserole dish. Cover with foil and bake for 45 to 55 minutes or until all the liquid is absorbed. Mix well and serve.

As a bonus, leftovers are great as a cold summer lunch.

Per serving: Calories 307.1, protein 11.8 g, total fat 3.7 g, carbohydrates 56.7 g, sodium 697.7 mg, fiber 8.7 g

TIP: Use this recipe as a template for a ton of easy quinoa dinners. Here are some examples:

Mexican: Substitute black or kidney beans for the chickpeas, add corn to the veggies or use a Mexican mix, season with cumin instead of basil and add ¼ to 1 teaspoon chili powder.

Indian: Replace the basil with garam masala and the oregano with ground coriander. Serve topped with chopped fresh cilantro.

MEXICAN KIDNEY BEAN FRIED RICE

• *gluten-free option** • *soy-free option*** • *oil-free option****

This is fusion cuisine at its quickest. I always have leftover cooked brown rice in the refrigerator, and sometimes I'm not in the mood for the Asian flavors of my go-to fried rice. Once I thought it over, I realized there's no reason not to add a Mexican flair to fried rice! This is good by itself or in tacos or burritos.

SERVES 6

2 tablespoons (30 ml) olive oil (***sauté in water instead)

¼ cup (40 g) minced onion (or 1 cup [151 g] julienned, if you love onions)

2 cups (184 g) julienned bell peppers

½ cup (35 g) shredded purple cabbage

1½ cups (367.5 g) mixed veggies or shredded meatless vegan chicken (*gluten-free and/or **soy-free)

1 (14.5 ounces [411 g]) can or 1½ cups (241 g) diced tomatoes

1 cup (240 g) crushed tomatoes (or 2 tablespoons [42 g] tomato paste plus ¾ cup [177 ml] water)

1 (15.5 ounce [440 g]) can kidney beans

1 cup (164 g) corn kernels

2 tablespoons (17 g) green chilies

1 tablespoon (1.6 g) oregano

1½ teaspoons (7 g) cumin

1 to 2 teaspoons chili powder, to taste

¼ to ½ teaspoon liquid smoke, to taste

3 cups (570 g) cooked brown rice

Salt, to taste

Heat the oil over medium-high heat. Once it's hot, add the onions and sauté until translucent, about 5 minutes.

Add the bell peppers and cabbage and sauté 3 more minutes. Turn down the heat to medium.

Add the mixed veggies or meatless chicken, tomatoes (diced and crushed), kidney beans, corn, green chilies, oregano, cumin, chili powder and liquid smoke. Cook until the veggies are tender and the flavors have melded, about 10 to 15 minutes, stirring every 5 minutes or so.

Turn the heat back up to medium-high and break up the cold cooked rice into the mixture. Keep stirring and cook until the rice is thoroughly heated, about 10 minutes.

Before serving, add salt to taste. Serve as is or in a burrito.

Per serving: Calories 375.8, protein 11.5 g, total fat 7.1 g, carbohydrates 73.5 g, sodium 454.7 mg, fiber 13.0 g

TIP: Make a Cajun-inspired variation by substituting DIY Cajun Seasoning Blend (page 30) for the chili powder and cumin. Leave out the green chilies, too.

HOLIDAY STUFFING CASSEROLE

• *gluten-free option** • *soy-free option*** • *oil-free option****

I always buy an extra bag of vegan stuffing around the holidays to stash in my pantry for this dish. It reminds me of a casserole my mom used to make that was topped with a layer of dressing. Underneath was a creamy filling. I use veggies and a vegan protein for that layer in my casserole.

SERVES 6

1 (10 oz [283 g]) bag vegan stuffing (*use gluten-free)

2 cups (340 g) mixed cauliflower, broccoli and carrots (or 1 [12 oz/340g] bag frozen California mix)

½ cup (124 g) green peas

½ cup (82 g) corn kernels

2 cups (480 g) **chickpeas, *crumbled tempeh or vegan meat-free chicken

1 teaspoon rubbed sage

1 teaspoon thyme

½ teaspoon salt

½ teaspoon rosemary

¼ teaspoon pepper

3 cups (708 g) vegan gravy ***DIY Golden Creamy Gravy (page 17)

Preheat the oven to 350°F (177°C) and either oil an 8.5" x 11" (21 x 28 cm) pan or ***line with parchment paper.

Cook the stuffing according to the directions on the package (***leave out the oil for oil-free). Set aside to cool.

Spread the mixed vegetables, peas, corn and protein of your choice evenly across the pan. One by one, measure out the herbs, salt and pepper and sprinkle over the pan.

Top the veggies with gravy as evenly as you can, then put the stuffing on top. Cover with foil, place pan on a baking sheet to catch drips and bake for 45 minutes. Uncover, then bake for 15 more minutes.

Per serving with chickpeas: Calories 361.0, protein 16.3 g, total fat 5.4 g, carbohydrates 63.5 g, sodium 1160.6 mg, fiber 10.6 g

RICHA'S CHICKPEA-STUFFED POBLANO PEPPERS WITH SMOKY TOMATO SAUCE

• gluten-free   • soy-free   • oil-free option*

My friend Richa Hingle, of VeganRicha.com, makes wonderful Indian fusion food. I asked her to share one of her recipes, and she chose this delicious stuffed poblano pepper with an Indian twist.

SERVES 2

FOR THE SMOKY TOMATO SAUCE

1 (14.5 oz [411 g]) can diced tomatoes

½ roasted red bell pepper

¼ cup (60 ml) water

2 cloves garlic, minced

2 teaspoons (4 g) grated ginger

½ teaspoon smoked paprika

½ teaspoon garam masala

½ teaspoon turmeric powder

¼ teaspoon salt, or to taste

¼ teaspoon cayenne powder, or to taste

¼ cup (50 g) chickpeas

2 tablespoons (18 g) cashews

1 teaspoon olive oil (*or sauté in water)

FOR THE STUFFING

1¼ cups (250 g) chickpeas

¼ teaspoon salt

¼ to ½ teaspoon cayenne, or to taste

¼ teaspoon garam masala

¼ cup (4 g) finely chopped cilantro

¼ teaspoon cumin powder

Olive oil as needed (optional)

2 large poblano peppers

GARNISHES

Chopped fresh cilantro

A sprinkle of paprika

A squeeze of lemon juice

Preheat the oven to 400°F (204°C) and line a baking sheet with parchment paper.

Add all the tomato sauce ingredients to a blender and blend to a smooth purée. Take out 2 tablespoons (30 ml) of the sauce and set the rest aside.

Take the 2 tablespoons (30 ml) of the tomato sauce and mix in the 1¼ cups (250 g) of chickpeas. Add salt, cayenne, garam masala and cilantro, then mash and mix. Taste and adjust salt and spice.

Slice the poblanos in half and remove seeds. Fill the peppers with the mashed chickpea mixture. Sprinkle cumin powder on top of each half. Spray or brush the peppers with oil if using.

Bake for 20 minutes or until the peppers start browning on the edges.

While the peppers are baking, heat a sauté pan to medium heat. Add the remaining tomato mixture from the blender and bring to a boil.

Lower the heat to medium-low and cook for another 6 to 7 minutes, or until the sauce thickens slightly. Taste and adjust salt and spice if needed.

Serve with a generous drizzle of the cooked tomato sauce and a sprinkle of sweet paprika, cilantro and lemon juice.

Per serving without sauce: Calories 193.5, protein 7.4 g, total fat 1.7 g, carbohydrates 33.9 g, sodium 448.5 mg, fiber 6.6 g

Per serving with oil: Calories 156.4, protein 3.6 g, total fat 2.7 g, carbohydrates 16.4 g, sodium 421.2 mg, fiber 3.7 g

CARROT AND KALE FALAFEL

• *gluten-free* • *soy-free* • *oil-free option**

Falafel has always had a special place in my heart. I love those little patties; I practically lived off them during my time in New York. They are slightly crispy on the outside and moist on the inside. Mine have the usual base of chickpeas, but they kick the veggies up a notch with carrots and kale. With a food processor, you can have them ready to bake in minutes. Serve as a main course with a side of hummus and a salad, on pita bread as a sandwich, or chop up and use on the Falafel "Pitza" on page 159.

MAKES 23 PATTIES

1 cup (128 g) chopped or shredded carrots

¼ cup (40 g) chopped onion

2 cloves garlic

½ cup (34 g) chopped kale (about 1 medium leaf)

½ cup (30 g) chopped parsley

2 tablespoons (30 ml) olive oil (*substitute tahini or pumpkin purée)

1 tablespoon (15 ml) lemon juice

1 tablespoon (15 g) tahini

1½ teaspoons (7 g) cumin

1 (15 oz [425 g]) can chickpeas, rinsed and drained or 1½ cups (300 g) cooked

3 to 4 tablespoons (30 to 40 g) brown rice flour (or whole-wheat or gluten-free baking mix)

½ teaspoon salt or salt, to taste

Preheat the oven to 350°F (177°C). Line a large baking sheet with parchment paper.

Add the carrots, onion and garlic to your food processor and process until very small pieces remain. Add the kale and parsley and process until minced.

Now add the olive oil, lemon juice, tahini, cumin and chickpeas and process some more. You want the chickpeas to have a little texture and not be smooth like hummus.

Add 3 tablespoons (30 g) of the flour and salt and process until just mixed in. If the batter is too thin, add the remaining flour.

I make the patties using a 1-tablespoon scoop and then flatten them slightly with the back of a spoon or my hand. You can make larger patties, but you will need to increase the cooking time.

Bake for 10 minutes, then flip and bake 10 minutes more. These will keep for about 5 days in the refrigerator, or you can freeze the leftovers for a busy night.

Per patty with oil: Calories 37.5, protein 1.1 g, total fat 1.7 g, carbohydrates 4.7 g, sodium 52.9 mg, fiber 1.0 g

TIP: Want larger patties? Recipe tester and photographer Ann says, "If you use a ¼-cup measure for the batter, you'll get about 10 patties and you'll need to cook them for about 30 minutes instead of 20." Thanks, Ann!

APPLE-BRAISED TEMPEH AND BUTTERNUT SQUASH BAKE

• *gluten-free* • *soy-free option** • *no oil added*

While this dish does need an hour of cooking time, it comes together quickly, making it a great choice for a night when you aren't in the mood to cook anything fussy. Cut up a few things, add your favorite vegetable broth and toss it in the oven. That leaves you an hour to use as you please. Just be sure to set a timer and don't go too far, since you'll remove the foil 20 minutes in.

SERVES 4

1 (8-ounce [226g]) package tempeh, cut into large cubes (*15 oz [425 g] can of chickpeas, drained and rinsed)

1 large apple, cut into large cubes

1 pound (454 g) bag frozen butternut squash cut into cubes

¼ cup (40 g) chopped onion

3 cloves garlic, sliced

2 cups (470 ml) vegetable broth (or water with 1 bouillon cube)

2 bay leaves

2 teaspoons (10 ml) vegan Worcestershire sauce

2 teaspoons (10 g) thyme

1 teaspoon rosemary

½ teaspoon salt

¼ teaspoon pepper

Rice (or your favorite grain), to serve

Dreamy Greens (page 170)

Preheat oven to 400°F (204°C).

Evenly spread the tempeh, apple, butternut squash, onion and garlic cloves in an 8½" x 11" (21 x 28 cm) casserole dish.

Mix the remaining ingredients, then pour over the contents of the baking dish.

Cover with foil and bake 20 minutes; then uncover and cook about 40 more minutes, until the apples are tender.

Serve over your favorite grain, with a side of Dreamy Greens (page 170).

Per serving: Calories 210.1, protein 11.4 g, total fat 5.7 g, carbohydrates 30.8 g, sodium 545.7 mg, fiber 9.3 g

CREAMY BROCCOLI AND POTATO CASSEROLE

• *gluten-free*   • *soy-free*   • *oil-free option**

This casserole is like a creamy stuffed broccoli baked potato. You can add any of the extras you like on a potato, such as sautéed mushrooms or shredded vegan cheese. The only limit is your imagination.

SERVES 4

4 cups (624 g) chopped potato

1 head broccoli, chopped, about 4 cups (364 g)

1½ cups (375 g) Almond Ricotta (page 24) or Cauliflower Ricotta (page 34)

1 cup (240 ml) nondairy milk

3 tablespoons (45 ml) unsweetened vegan yogurt + 2 tablespoons (12 g) nutritional yeast, or 3 tablespoons (45 ml) Carrot Cashew Chez (page 27)

½ teaspoon salt

½ teaspoon black pepper

Chives or scallions, for serving

Preheat the oven to 350°F (177°C) and either oil an 8½" x 11" (21 x 28 cm) casserole dish or *line it with parchment paper.

Mix all of the ingredients except the chives or scallions in a large mixing bowl. Then transfer to the prepared casserole dish and cover with foil.

Bake for 45 to 60 minutes or until the potatoes are easily pierced with a fork.

Serve with chives or scallions sprinkled on top.

Per serving: Calories 160.2, protein 7.5 g, total fat 1.7 g, carbohydrates 31.7 g, sodium 102.3 mg, fiber 8.0 g

TIP: Make it heartier by adding a 15 ounce (425 g) can of chickpeas or equivalent amount of tempeh crumbles.

SWEET POTATO ROPA VIEJA

• *gluten-free*   • *soy-free*   • *oil-free option**

In this stew that's named "old clothes," we use shredded sweet potatoes in place of the traditional beef. This recipe was inspired by one of Robin Robertson's that stars shredded sweet potatoes. I love how they hold their shape in this bold stew. It's hard to believe, but they do not get mushy at all and their flavor is not in the foreground either.

SERVES 6

1 to 2 tablespoons (15-30 ml) olive oil (*sauté in water instead)

¾ cup (120 g) chopped onion

4 cloves garlic, minced

¾ cup (112 g) chopped bell pepper

4 cups (600 g) peeled and shredded sweet potato (use your food processor if you have a shredding blade)

1 (28 oz [794 g]) can of crushed tomatoes

1 cup (237 ml) vegetable broth

1 tablespoon (15 ml) white or apple cider vinegar

2 bay leaves

2 teaspoons (10 g) oregano

1½ teaspoons (7 g) cumin

1½ teaspoons (7 g) salt

1 teaspoon thyme

½ teaspoon black pepper

Heat the olive oil in a large pot over medium-high heat. Once hot, add the onions and sauté until translucent, about 5 minutes. Then add the garlic and bell pepper and sauté 3 to 5 more minutes, until the peppers soften.

Add the rest of the ingredients, turn down heat to medium-low, cover and cook 15 to 20 minutes or until the sweet potato is soft enough to eat. Please note that the sweet potato will still have texture unlike a chopped sweet potato that cooks down, so it will retain the shredded look, but still be tender.

Serve over rice, in a burrito shell or just as it is, in a bowl.

Per serving with oil: Calories 173.5, protein 4.1 g, total fat 3.0 g, carbohydrates 35.2 g, sodium 344.3 mg, fiber 5.8 g

BAKED MAPLE SMOKED TEMPEH

• gluten-free   • soy-free option   • oil-free option*

This dish is sweet, salty and smoky—all of my favorite flavors at the same time. I like to pair it with Rosemary Roasted Potatoes and Beets (page 124). You can cook them both in the oven at the same temperature and relax while they both bake.

SERVES 4

½ cup (118 ml) vegetable broth

2 tablespoons (30 ml) maple syrup

½ teaspoon thyme

½ teaspoon sage

½ teaspoon salt (less if you use a salty broth)

¼ teaspoon garlic powder

¼ teaspoon liquid smoke

¼ teaspoon black pepper

Pinch cayenne pepper, optional

1 (8 oz [255 g]) package tempeh, cut into cubes

Preheat oven to 400°F (204°C). Oil an oven-safe baking dish (*or skip the oil and soak the pan overnight to make it easier to clean).

Combine all the ingredients in the baking dish and mix well.

Bake until the liquid is mostly absorbed and the tempeh is heated through and flavorful. This will take about 20 to 25 minutes.

Serve with your favorite veggies or maybe even over a bed of grits.

Per serving: Calories 148.0, protein 10.0 g, total fat 5.5 g, carbohydrates 15.1 g, sodium 124.0 mg, fiber 4.5 g

TIP: Slice the tempeh thin and put in the marinade. Then panfry for a great thin bean substitute.

ROSEMARY ROASTED POTATOES AND BEETS

• *gluten-free* • *soy-free* • *oil-free option**

This easy side dish cooks while you make the rest of your dinner. Everyone likes crispy potatoes, and you can mix in any other root veggies that came in your CSA, such as turnips, radishes or—my favorite!—beets. Pair this with Baked Maple Smoked Tempeh (page 123) for a complete meal.

SERVES 4

6 cups (900 g) diced potatoes

3 cups (408 g) diced beets (or other root veggie of your choice)

2 tablespoons (30 ml) olive oil (*leave out)

1½ teaspoons (7 g) rosemary

½ teaspoon salt

¼ teaspoon pepper

Preheat the oven to 400°F (204°C). Line a large baking sheet with parchment paper.

Add all the ingredients to a mixing bowl and toss to coat the veggies with the herbs and olive oil (if using).

Spread in a single layer over the baking sheet and roast for 20 to 30 minutes until the outsides are crispy. Be sure to stir the veggies around every 10 minutes so they will cook evenly.

Per serving with oil: Calories 258.8, protein 5.4 g, total fat 7.0 g, carbohydrates 45.1 g, sodium 115.4 mg, fiber 8.2 g

TIP: Roast the beets on a separate sheet pan if you don't want the red to bleed onto the potatoes. Personally, I like it when they mingle, but I adore beets!

APPLE ZUCCHINI BUCKWHEAT PANCAKES

• gluten-free • soy-free option • oil-free option***

Did you know that buckwheat is gluten-free? There's something about the earthy flavor and the dark pancakes that make me think of fall, but they are good any time of the year. These are a delicious way to use up the last of your zucchini while adding in a fresh-picked apple. Plus, you get to have breakfast for dinner!

MAKES 6 PANCAKES

DRY INGREDIENTS

1 cup (120 g) buckwheat flour

1 tablespoon (1.6 g) cinnamon

1 teaspoon baking powder

½ teaspoon allspice

¼ teaspoon nutmeg

¼ teaspoon salt

WET INGREDIENTS

1½ cups (355 ml) soy milk
(*use other nondairy milk)

1 teaspoon apple cider vinegar

2 tablespoons (14 g) ground flaxseed mixed with 4 tablespoons (59 ml) warm water

1 cup (124 g) shredded zucchini

½ cup (62 g) shredded apple

2 tablespoons (30 ml) olive oil
(**use applesauce or mashed banana)

Maple syrup, to serve

Nondairy butter, to serve (optional)

Mix the dry ingredients together in a medium-sized mixing bowl and set aside. Add the vinegar to the milk. It will curdle if you use soy milk, making a faux buttermilk. Mix the ground flaxseed with the warm water in a small bowl; it will thicken.

Add in the rest of the wet ingredients to the flax mixture.

Start heating your pancake pan over medium-low heat. Lightly coat the pan with olive or coconut oil. (*Use a nonstick pan.)

While the pan is heating, add the wet ingredients to the dry and mix until well combined. Drop about ½ cup (118 ml) of batter per pancake.

Cook for about 4 minutes or until you see the edges get dry. Flip and cook about 2 or 3 minutes more.

Serve with maple syrup and, if desired, some nondairy butter.

Per pancake with oil: Calories 139.3, protein 3.9 g, total fat 7.6 g, carbohydrates 15.1 g, sodium 128.2 mg, fiber 5.5 g

TIPS: When making larger pancakes like these, I use two skillets simultaneously to cut my time in front of the stove in half.

Don't limit yourself to zucchini and apple. Try adding berries in the spring, pears in the fall and carrots any time.

CHAPTER 6

SPEEDY STIR-FRIES

What I love most about stir-fries is that usually you just mix up a quick sauce, toss some cut-up veggies into a hot pan and go. Dinner is ready in a flash.

The secret to making the process easier is to cut up your veggies ahead of time. You can even use frozen vegetables that someone else cut for you!

I've included a few of my Chinese take-out favorites, and they are all veganed-up, of course: Pepper Portabella (page 135), Szechuan Eggplant (page 136) and more. Just say "no" to takeout, and make it yourself in the time it would take to drive there and back.

ORANGE GINGER CAULIFLOWER

• *gluten-free option** • *soy-free option***

This dish is half roasted and half stir-fried. The cauliflower gets lightly tossed with brown rice flour and roasted while you make the slightly sweet orange ginger sauce. Then you heat the sauce, add the cooked cauliflower and watch your sauce thicken up fast.

SERVES 4

½ cup (79 g) brown rice flour

2 tablespoons (15 g) tapioca starch (or 4 tablespoons [32 g] cornstarch)

2 tablespoons (12 g) nutritional yeast

½ teaspoon salt

1 head cauliflower, broken into small florets

SAUCE INGREDIENTS

1 cup (237 ml) orange juice

¼ cup (60 ml) white wine

3 tablespoons (45 ml) soy sauce (*use gluten-free soy sauce or **coconut aminos)

2 tablespoons (30 ml) rice wine vinegar

2 tablespoons (42 g) agave nectar

1 heaping tablespoon (8 g) fresh grated ginger (or 1 to 2 teaspoons ground)

2 cloves garlic, minced

Cooked brown rice, for serving

Preheat your oven to 400°F (204°C). Line a large baking sheet with parchment paper and set aside.

In a large bowl, combine the brown rice flour, tapioca starch, nutritional yeast and salt, then mix well.

Rinse the cauliflower florets in water, then toss in the flour mixture. Arrange in one layer on the baking sheet and bake for 15 to 20 minutes or until you can easily pierce the thick part of the stem with a fork.

While the cauliflower is cooking, mix all the sauce ingredients in a measuring cup. Heat a large sauté pan, add the sauce and cook for 1 or 2 minutes, until heated.

Add the cauliflower and toss. This will thicken up the sauce. Take off the heat when it's just a little thinner than you like it. It will continue to thicken while you're serving it. Serve over steamed brown rice.

Per serving without rice: Calories 208.1, protein 7.2 g, total fat 1.0 g, carbohydrates 43.0 g, sodium 724.1 mg, fiber 5.3 g

BROCCOLI WITH SPICY GARLIC SAUCE

• *gluten-free option** • *soy-free option*** • *oil-free option****

This is my favorite Chinese take-out dish. The broccoli makes it virtuous, but the spicy garlic sauce is what keeps me coming back for more. It's easier than you think to make at home, and you can make it as spicy as you like!

MAKES 4 SERVINGS

FOR THE SAUCE

½ cup (118 g) vegetable broth or water

2 tablespoons (30 ml) soy sauce (*use gluten-free or **use coconut aminos instead)

2 tablespoons (30 ml) agave nectar or maple syrup

1 tablespoon (15 ml) sesame oil (***use tahini or leave out)

3 cloves garlic, minced

1 to 2 teaspoons red pepper flakes, to taste

1 to 2 tablespoons (15-30 ml) olive oil or vegetable oil (***sauté in water instead)

6 cups broccoli florets (or 1 [1 pound/454 g] bag frozen)

2 teaspoons (6.3 g) cornstarch

Rice, to serve

Mix the sauce ingredients in a measuring cup and set aside.

Heat the oil in a wok or large sauté pan over medium-high heat. Once the oil is hot, add the broccoli florets and sauté until they start to soften, about 3 to 5 minutes.

Mix in all but 2 tablespoons (30 ml) of the sauce. Then stir the cornstarch into the leftover sauce until there are no lumps; add to pan. Cook until the sauce thickens, about 3 to 5 minutes.

Serve over rice.

Per serving with oil, without rice: Calories 136.3, protein 4.6 g, total fat 7.3 g, carbohydrates 16.6 g, sodium 604.5 mg, fiber 4.1 g

TIP: If you like yours extra-saucy, make a double batch of the sauce. Also try making this with thin Japanese eggplant cut into strips or even with a mix of veggies and tofu cubes.

PEPPER PORTABELLA

• *gluten-free option** • *soy-free option*** • *oil-free option****

Stir-fries are just the thing for a speedy dinner. This one comes together quickly even though there's a little chopping involved. You can make your life very easy by chopping the veggies the night before or in the morning and keeping them in the refrigerator until you're ready to cook.

MAKES 4 SERVINGS

FOR THE SAUCE

½ cup (118 g) vegetable broth or water

2 tablespoons (30 ml) soy sauce (*use gluten-free or **use coconut aminos instead)

1 tablespoon (15 ml) rice wine vinegar

1 teaspoon grated ginger

3 cloves garlic, minced

1 to 2 tablespoons (15–30 ml) olive oil or vegetable oil (***sauté in water instead)

3 cups (110 g) julienned onion (about 1 large onion)

4 cups (296 g) julienned bell pepper (about 4 small bell peppers)

5 cups (430 g) sliced portabella (ribs removed, then sliced lengthwise in thick slices, then into ½ inch [⅓ cm] pieces)

1 teaspoon cornstarch

Rice, to serve (optional)

Mix the sauce ingredients in a measuring cup and set aside.

Heat the oil in a wok or large sauté pan over medium-high heat. Once the oil is hot, add the onions and sauté until they start to soften, about 3 minutes. Add the bell pepper and cook for 3 more minutes.

Add the portabellas and cook until they shrink and start to brown slightly, about 5 minutes. Mix in all but 2 tablespoons (30 ml) of the sauce.

Stir the cornstarch into the leftover sauce until there are no lumps, then add to the pan. Cook until the sauce thickens, about 3 to 5 minutes.

Serve over rice.

Per serving with oil, without rice: Calories 153.8, protein 6.0 g, total fat 4.1 g, carbohydrates 27.3 g, sodium 581.7 mg, fiber 5.5 g

SZECHUAN EGGPLANT

• *gluten-free option**   • *soy-free option***   • *oil-free option****

I'm a picky eggplant eater. I love it when it's cooked through, but when it's the least bit crunchy you can count me out. This was the first dish that really got me hooked on eggplant. It has a hearty texture and a rich flavor, cooked down and covered in a fragrant spicy hot sauce that takes no time to throw together.

MAKES 4 SERVINGS

FOR THE SAUCE

½ cup (118 g) vegetable broth or water

2 tablespoons (30 ml) soy sauce (*use gluten-free or **use coconut aminos instead)

1 tablespoon (15 ml) agave nectar or maple syrup

2 teaspoons (4 g) grated ginger

2 teaspoons to 1 tablespoon (10-15 ml) chili garlic sauce or sriracha, to taste

1 teaspoon sesame oil (***use tahini or leave out)

3 cloves garlic, minced

1 to 2 teaspoons red pepper flakes, to taste

1 to 2 tablespoons (15-30 ml) olive oil or vegetable oil (***sauté in water instead)

6 cups (492 g) eggplant chunks (about 1 large eggplant)

2 teaspoons (6.3 g) cornstarch

Rice, to serve

Mix the sauce ingredients in a measuring cup and set aside.

Heat the oil in a wok or large sauté pan over medium-high heat. Once the oil is hot, add the eggplant and sauté until soft, about 10 minutes. Its bright white color will turn brownish and then semitranslucent.

Mix in all but 2 tablespoons (30 ml) of the sauce. Then stir the cornstarch into the leftover sauce until there are no lumps and add it to the pan. Cook until the sauce thickens, about 3 minutes.

Serve over rice.

Per serving with oil, less rice: Calories 102.7, protein 1.9 g, total fat 4.7 g, carbohydrates 14.7 g, sodium 630.2 mg, fiber 3.2 g

ANN'S VEGETABLE FRIED RICE WITH TOFU

• *gluten-free option** • *soy-free option*** • *no oil added*

Ann Oliverio, author of *Crave, Eat, Heal*, makes a healthier version of fried rice. By cooking it at home, you can tweak it to your own tastes and add the veggies you have on hand. All you need to start with is some cold leftover rice, so be sure to make extra next time you cook up a batch.

MAKES 4 SERVINGS

4 cups (780 g) cooked cold brown rice

1 cup (237 ml) vegetable broth or water, as needed

1 small onion, chopped

1 large bell pepper, cored, seeded and chopped

2 cups (268 g) asparagus, cut into 1-inch (2.5-cm) pieces

1 tablespoon (8.5 g) garlic, minced

1 tablespoon (6 g) fresh grated ginger

2 cups (504 g) baked tofu, cut into ½-inch (1.3-cm) pieces

¼ cup (60 ml) dry sherry, optional

4 tablespoons (60 ml) soy sauce (*use gluten-free or **coconut aminos)

Salt and pepper, to taste

¼ cup (4 g) chopped cilantro

4 scallions, chopped

¼ cup (36 g) chopped roasted peanuts, for serving

Quartered limes, for serving

Hot sauce, for serving

Heat a large skillet or wok over high heat. Splash ¼ cup (60 ml) vegetable broth into it and add the onion and bell pepper. Lower heat a little and stir, adding more broth as needed. Cook for about 5 minutes, letting the broth cook off so that the vegetables brown a little. Remove them to a bowl or plate and set aside.

Add ¼ cup (60 ml) broth to the pan, then add the asparagus pieces, cooking just until they turn bright green. Add them to the veggie mixture you have set aside.

Add 2 tablespoons (30 ml) of broth to the pan and the garlic and ginger, stirring only for about half a minute or so. Add the rice a bit at a time, breaking up any clumps. Stir and add broth as needed to keep from scorching.

Once you have all of the rice in the pan, stir until it starts sticking a bit. Now add the tofu and cooked veggies along with the sherry. Cook for about 1 minute.

Add the soy sauce, salt and pepper. Turn off the heat and add the scallions. Divide rice among four big bowls and top with cilantro, peanuts and limes.

Per serving with peanuts: Calories 538.9, protein 30.1 g, total fat 13.1 g, carbohydrates 76.0 g, sodium 1810.5 mg, fiber 10.7 g

TIP: No sherry? Try rice wine vinegar instead.

CHAPTER 7

EASY SANDWICH FILLINGS AND SPREADS

Who doesn't love a sandwich? They're quick and easy, and there is endless variety.

In this chapter, I have included one of the most popular recipes from my blog: All-Natural Carrot Dogs (page 147). These are carrots that have been marinated to come pretty close to the flavor of a hot dog. Drunken Sweet Potato BBQ (page 156) will shake things up at your next party; I love that all the hard preparation can be done with your food processor. It's made with shredded sweet potatoes and a hard cider bourbon barbeque sauce that takes no time to whip up. There's also a southern-style quesadilla (page 143), Brussels sprout tacos (page 148), a cauliflower po' boy with spicy vegan mayo (page 151) and much more. You'll find yourself looking forward to sandwich night!

CREAMY BLACK-EYED PEA SOUTHERN QUESADILLAS

• gluten-free option* • soy-free • no oil added

Tired of the same old quesadillas? Try adding some of this creamy and smoky black-eyed pea Cajun-spiced filling. These come together quickly. Don't let the number of spices put you off; that's what makes this filling sparkle.

MAKES 4 QUESADILLAS

1½ cups (200 g) chopped sweet potato (peeled if not organic) or puréed pumpkin

1 (15 oz [425 g]) can of black-eyed peas, rinsed and drained or 1½ cups (295 g) home-cooked black-eyed peas

1 teaspoon thyme

1 teaspoon paprika

½ teaspoon garlic powder

¼ to ½ teaspoon cayenne pepper, to taste

⅛ teaspoon allspice

salt and pepper, to taste

hot sauce of choice, to taste

¼ cup (65.5 g) plain vegan yogurt or Cashew Sour Cream (page 22)

3 tablespoons (15 g) nutritional yeast

A few drops liquid smoke

Whole-wheat flour tortillas (*use gluten-free tortillas)

Your favorite salsa, for serving

Place the sweet potatoes in a saucepan and cover with water. Bring to a boil, then lower to medium heat. Simmer until a fork can easily pierce the potato, about 10 minutes. Drain in a strainer. If you use pumpkin purée, you can skip this step.

Add the sweet potato or pumpkin, black-eyed peas, thyme, paprika, garlic powder, cayenne and allspice and mash well until the beans are smashed into the mix. Add salt, pepper and hot sauce to taste.

Mix in the yogurt or Cashew Sour Cream and liquid smoke. Taste and adjust seasonings if needed.

Heat skillet over medium heat.

Spread the bean mixture on one tortilla and top with another. Cook in the skillet about 4 to 5 minutes on each side. Serve with your favorite salsa on the side.

Per serving without salsa: Calories 183.6, protein 4.9 g, total fat 3.0 g, carbohydrates 33.1 g, sodium 21 mg, fiber 5.7 g

TIP: The longer the skillet is hot, the more quickly the quesadillas will cook. Therefore, the last one will take less time than the first one.

SLOPPY 'SHROOMS

• gluten-free • soy-free • no oil added

These mushrooms are cooked in a tangy sauce and bulked up with quinoa for even more protein. This stew is great over an open-faced toasted whole-wheat bun. It's easy to throw together in the slow cooker in the morning so you can come home to a ready-to-eat dinner.

SERVES 4

3 cups (8.25 oz [234 g]) mushrooms, chopped small

½ teaspoon minced garlic

½ medium red bell pepper, minced

1 medium carrot, minced or shredded

½ cup (3 oz [86 g]) quinoa, rinsed and drained

2½ cups (591 ml) water

1 veggie bouillon cube or 1 tablespoon (5 g) nutritional yeast

2 tablespoons (33 g) tomato paste

1 teaspoon apple cider vinegar

1 teaspoon vegan Worcestershire sauce

1 teaspoon paprika

1 teaspoon oregano

1 teaspoon tarragon

½ teaspoon coriander

½ teaspoon salt, to taste

¼ teaspoon black pepper

½ cup (33.5 g) minced kale or other greens

Toasted buns or baked potatoes, to serve

STOVE-TOP METHOD

In a soup pot on medium heat, stir the mushrooms until they start to release their liquid. Add the garlic, pepper and carrot. Cook for about 5 minutes.

Add the rest of the ingredients except for the kale, stir and bring to a boil. Lower the heat to medium-low and cover. Simmer for 10 to 15 minutes, until the quinoa is tender.

Stir in the kale and serve over toasted buns or baked potatoes.

SLOW COOKER METHOD

Combine everything but the kale in a 4-quart (4-L) slow cooker and cook on low for 7 to 9 hours. Stir in the kale right before serving. Taste and adjust seasonings and serve.

Per serving: Calories 120.1, protein 6.4 g, total fat 1.6 g, carbohydrates 22.0 g, sodium 119.4 mg, fiber 3.8 g

ALL-NATURAL CARROT DOGS

• *gluten-free* • *soy-free* • *oil-free option**

A carrot is the same shape as a hot dog and close enough in color to make a decent substitute. But what about the taste? I promise you, this marinade really takes it to the next level. I think the sesame oil helps, but the vinegar gives it that "cured" flavor, too.

SERVES 4

4 carrots, cut into bun lengths

¼ cup (60 ml) seasoned rice vinegar (or apple cider vinegar and a dash of salt)

¼ cup (60 ml) water

1 tablespoon (15 ml) sesame oil (*leave out)

2 tablespoons (30 ml) coconut aminos (can substitute soy sauce; use unseasoned vinegar)

¼ teaspoon garlic powder (or ½ clove garlic, minced)

¼ teaspoon liquid smoke

Pepper, to taste

Toasted hot dog bun, lettuce or collard leaves, to serve

Heat water in a pot large enough for all the carrots. When it comes to a boil, turn down to medium heat and add the carrots. Cook until you can just pierce them through with a fork; you want them to have a snap when you bite into them. Remove from pot and run cold water over them to stop them from cooking.

In a container with a tight-fitting lid, combine the remaining ingredients to make the marinade. Tighten the lid and shake until well mixed.

Place the carrots in a container in which they can lie flat. Pour the marinade over them and marinate at least 3 to 4 hours, up to 24. The longer they marinate, the more vinegar flavor they take on. If you know you need to leave them longer than a day, cut the vinegar to ⅛ cup (30 ml). If the carrots are very skinny, keep the marinating time short.

To serve, heat the carrots in a 350°F (177°C) oven, or in a grill pan on a hot grill, until heated through, 10 to 15 minutes.

Serve in a toasted hot dog bun or wrapped in a lettuce or collard leaf, and pile on your favorite toppings.

Per serving with oil: Calories 92.1, protein 0.7 g, total fat 3.5 g, carbohydrates 17.3 g, sodium 749.7 mg, fiber 2.0 g

TIP: You can cook these in your slow cooker in the marinade. You need to check on them so they do not get mushy, so it is not a set-it-and-walk-away affair. Cook until a fork just goes through the carrot but it is still slightly firm.

DELIGHTFUL BRUSSELS SPROUT TACOS

• gluten-free   • soy-free   • oil-free option*

Every autumn, I'm drawn to the three-foot-long stalks of Brussels sprouts I see in the stores and markets. I start throwing sprouts in everything. After I slice and sauté them in cumin and chili powder, they are the perfect texture for the base of a taco. Top with lettuce, chopped tomatoes, Cashew Sour Cream and salsa!

MAKES 8 TO 10 TACOS

1 to 2 tablespoons (15-30 ml) olive oil (*sauté in water instead)

1½ teaspoons (7 g) cumin

½ to 1 teaspoon chili powder, to taste

3 cloves garlic, minced

2½ cups (220 g) Brussels sprouts, sliced thin or shredded

Salt, to taste

FOR SERVING

Taco shells

Lettuce

Tomatoes

Cashew Sour Cream (page 22) with a squeeze of lime juice

Salsa

Heat the olive oil (*or water) in a large sauté pan over medium heat. Add the cumin, chili powder and garlic and sauté for about 3 minutes, until the spices become fragrant.

Add the Brussels sprouts and sauté until tender, stirring constantly, about 10 to 13 minutes. Before serving, add salt to taste. Assemble as you wish.

Per serving with oil, without shells: Calories 28.4, protein 1.0 g, total fat 1.8 g, carbohydrates 2.8 g, sodium 7.1 mg, fiber 1.1 g

TIP 1: Why not try other single-veggie taco fillings? Cubed summer squash adds a punch of color. Don't forget the Cauliflower Mexi Mince on page 18.

TIP 2: Buy pre-shredded Brussels sprouts to cut out the hard work and you'll have them on the table even sooner.

SPICY (OR NOT) CAULIFLOWER PO' BOY

• gluten-free option* • soy-free • oil-free option**

Living in New Orleans makes you think anything can be made into a sandwich. After all, if you can have a French fry po' boy, why not one made of cauliflower? Please note that the cauliflower will be bone dry after it's roasted, so it will need to be "dressed" in some kind of saucy condiment. In New Orleans, if you order a sandwich "dressed," that means you want mayo, lettuce and tomato.

SERVES 4

½ head cauliflower, broken into florets

½ loaf soft French bread, cut into 4 pieces depending on loaf size (*use gluten-free bread)

DRY MIX

½ cup (62.5 g) white whole-wheat flour or regular whole wheat (*use a gluten-free flour blend)

¼ cup (30.5 g) cornmeal

1 tablespoon (5 g) DIY Cajun Seasoning Blend (page 30)

2 teaspoons (3.3 g) nutritional yeast

1 teaspoon salt

½ teaspoon smoked paprika

¼ teaspoon black pepper

WET MIX

2 tablespoons (30 ml) unsweetened nondairy milk

1 tablespoon (15 ml) not-too-hot vinegar-based hot sauce such as Texas Pete or Louisiana Hot Sauce

SPICY MAYO

¼ cup (60 g) vegan mayo or Cashew Sour Cream (page 22)

1½ teaspoons (7 ml) garlic Tabasco or the hot sauce you used in the wet mix

½ teaspoon dijon mustard

Preheat the oven to 350°F (177°C). Spray a large sheet pan with oil (**or line with parchment paper). Set aside.

Combine the dry mix ingredients in a small mixing bowl and the wet ones in a separate bowl. Toss the cauliflower florets in the wet mixture then transfer to the dry mixture and coat well.

Spread the florets on the sheet pan and roast for 20 to 30 minutes, turning every 10 minutes. Cook until the cauliflower is tender and is easily pierced with a fork.

While the cauliflower roasts, mix the mayo ingredients together. If the French bread is fresh there is no need to toast it, but if it's getting dry, go ahead and toast it.

Spread a thick layer of the spicy mayo (**use mustard or tofu sour cream) on both sides of the bread, then layer with the cooked cauliflower. You can top with more hot sauce, lettuce and tomato.

Per serving: Calories 35.6, protein 0.0 g, total fat 3.5 g, carbohydrates 0.0 g, sodium 131.9 mg, fiber 0.0 g

Per serving with bread: Calories 261.1, protein 9.1 g, total fat 2.6 g, carbohydrates 49.9 g, sodium 476.8 mg, fiber 4.5 g

TIP: These are addictive. Make a double batch and freeze some for another time. Just reheat in a 350°F (177°C) oven until warm.

PUMPKIN HUMMUS

• gluten-free   • soy-free   • no oil added

Hummus is a vegan staple. It gets a bad rap because sometimes it's a vegan's only friend at a party. But hummus does not have to be boring, especially if you up the flavor with pumpkin, smoked paprika, cumin and a little nutritional yeast. Try this as a base on the Falafel "Pitza" on page 159.

MAKES ABOUT 2½ CUPS (301 G)

1 (15 oz [425 g]) can chickpeas, rinsed and drained or 1½ cups (300 g) cooked

¾ cup (184 g) pumpkin purée (can substitute sweet potato or butternut squash purée)

2 cloves garlic, sliced

1 tablespoon (15 ml) lemon juice

2 tablespoons (10 g) nutritional yeast

½ to 1 teaspoon cumin, to taste

¼ teaspoon smoked paprika

¼ to ½ teaspoon coriander, to taste, optional

¼ teaspoon cayenne

2 to 3 tablespoons (30 to 45 ml) water, as needed, to make a smooth purée

Salt, to taste

Place the chickpeas, pumpkin, garlic, lemon juice, nutritional yeast, cumin, paprika, coriander and cayenne in your food processor. Blend until the chickpeas are puréed. Add a tablespoon (15 ml) of water at a time if the mixture is too thick.

Taste and adjust seasonings; add salt to taste.

Per ½ cup (60 g) serving: Calories 107.5, protein 5.4 g, total fat 1.0 g, carbohydrates 20.2 g, sodium 217.0 mg, fiber 5.1 g

MIDDLE EASTERN CHICKPEA SALAD

• gluten-free   • soy-free option*   • oil-free

Some nights you need something beyond easy. Think of these cumin-spiced chickpeas as cheater falafel. Here, they're slathered in vegan yogurt and mixed with chunky tomatoes, crunchy cucumbers and green peppers.

SERVES 4

1 (15 oz [425 g]) can chickpeas, rinsed and drained or 1½ cups (300 g) cooked

½ cup (113 g) unsweetened nondairy yogurt (substitute *Cashew Sour Cream [page 22] or vegan mayo)

¼ cup (45 g) diced tomatoes

¼ cup (34 g) diced cucumbers

¼ cup (15 g) minced parsley

2 tablespoons (18 g) diced bell pepper

½ teaspoon granulated garlic

1 teaspoon cumin

1 teaspoon coriander

½ teaspoon paprika

Salt and pepper, to taste

Pinch of sumac, optional

Pita bread, for serving (gluten-free if you need)

Lettuce leaves, for serving

Mash the chickpeas in a mixing bowl with a potato masher or fork. Then stir in the yogurt, tomatoes, cucumbers, parsley, bell pepper, granulated garlic, cumin, coriander and paprika.

Taste the mixture, adjust seasonings and add salt and pepper to taste. Serve in pita bread with lettuce.

Per serving: Calories 125.3, protein 4.7 g, total fat 2.1 g, carbohydrates 22.9 g, sodium 320.6 mg, fiber 5.2 g

DRUNKEN SWEET POTATO BBQ

• gluten-free option* *• soy-free* *• no oil added*

There's nothing better than a tangy BBQ sandwich. This recipe was inspired by one from Robin Robertson, in which she uses shredded sweet potatoes. I had thought that, when shredded, sweet potatoes would turn to mush like they do when they're cut into chunks, but they actually stand up well and keep their texture. My BBQ sauce combines hard cider and coconut sugar with tomato paste and just a hint of bourbon. It's a rich sauce that's a little sweet, a little tangy and a little smoky. Why not make up a batch to use on veggie burgers while you're at it?

MAKES 8 SANDWICHES

1 (12 oz [355 ml]) bottle hard cider (*be sure it's labeled "gluten-free")

¼ cup (36 g) coconut or brown sugar

¼ cup (65 g) tomato paste

1 tablespoon (21 g) molasses

1 teaspoon bourbon, optional (*be sure it's labeled "gluten-free")

½ teaspoon salt

¼ teaspoon garlic powder

¼ teaspoon liquid smoke

⅛ to 1 teaspoon cayenne pepper, to taste

4 cups (532 g) peeled and shredded sweet potato (1 really large or 2 to 3 medium ones—shred using your food processor's smaller shredding disc)

½ cup (118 ml) water, if needed

TO SERVE (OPTIONAL)

Buns or toast

Coleslaw

Corn on the cob

Pour the hard cider into a Dutch oven or soup pot, then whisk in the sugar, tomato paste, molasses and bourbon (if using). Bring to a boil, then turn heat down to medium and simmer for about 10 minutes. The mixture will reduce a bit.

Stir in the salt, garlic powder, liquid smoke and cayenne.

Add the sweet potatoes, mix well, turn heat to medium-low and cover. Cook for 10 minutes, then stir. Add the ½ cup (118 ml) of water if the sauce has reduced too much for the sweet potatoes to keep cooking.

Cook 10 more minutes, and the sweet potatoes will be tender. They will not be mushy, but more like al dente pasta.

Serve on a bun, over toast or as a "plate" with coleslaw and corn on the cob.

Per sandwich: Calories 252.0, protein 2.9 g, total fat 0.5 g, carbohydrates 56.7 g, sodium 154.3 mg, fiber 4.7 g

TIP: Try crumbled tempeh in place of the sweet potato for a change.

FALAFEL "PITZA"

• *gluten-free option** • *soy-free* • *no oil added*

I got the idea for this pita-pizza combo from a local Middle Eastern restaurant. They spread a tahini sauce on top of thin pita bread, then crumble falafel on it and top with veggies. I try to make these the same week I make the Carrot and Kale Falafel recipe on page 115 as a tasty way to use up the leftovers.

. . . .

SERVES 4

. . . .

FOR THE TAHINI SAUCE

½ cup (113 g) tahini

¼ cup (65.5 g) vegan plain yogurt, unsweetened if possible, or Cashew Sour Cream (page 22)

1 to 2 tablespoons (15–30 ml) lemon juice, to taste

4 whole-wheat pitas (*use gluten-free)

4 to 8 pieces of falafel, chopped (recipe on page 115)

1 cup (180 g) chopped tomato

½ cup (62 g) chopped pickled banana peppers

1 cup (133 g) chopped cucumber

Handful of chopped parsley, for garnish

A few pinches of sumac, optional

Preheat the oven to 375°F (177°C). Lay out two baking sheets. You will not need to oil them or use parchment paper.

Mix the ingredients for the tahini sauce and spread on the top of each pita round. Layer on the chopped falafel, tomatoes and banana peppers and bake until the toppings are hot and the pita gets toasted, about 10 to 15 minutes.

Once you remove them from the oven, top with the cucumber, parsley and a pinch of sumac. I also drizzle any leftover tahini sauce on top.

. . . .

Per serving: Calories 436.0, protein 14.3 g, total fat 22.0 g, carbohydrates 52.5 g, sodium 455.3 mg, fiber 9.8 g

. . . .

TIP: This recipe is a great way to get rid of that leftover bit of hummus: just use it in place of the tahini spread. Try it topped with shredded carrots or raw veggies for extra crunch.

STRAIGHT-FORWARD SIDES

I'm including a few sides here so your stews and sandwiches don't get lonely. I know that when you're in a hurry, it's easy to skip adding anything else to a meal.

Here are Zucchini Masala Fries (page 167), Sweet Potato Fries with Parsley, Garlic and Lemon Zest (page 173), and Baked Crispy Breaded Green Beans (page 168) that will satisfy your cravings and turn that snack into a satisfying meal.

Then there's the recipe for Dreamy Greens (page 170), which can be made into a meal with just a few easy changes. Spicy Creamed Corn (page 174) is a nice side for any Mexican meal, but it's also a perfect appetizer dip that you can keep warm in your slow cooker.

Finally, there are exciting drop biscuits flavored with veggies (page 163), and one even contains quinoa (page 164). Since they're drop biscuits, you won't have to roll out or cut the dough! Try them with Maple Walnut Sausage Patties (page 35) or pair with one of the soups in Chapter 2.

WHOLE-WHEAT PUMPKIN ROSEMARY DROP BISCUITS

• gluten-free option * • soy-free option***

Delicious and hearty drop biscuits are common throughout the South, but they are usually laden with animal products, unhealthy fats and highly processed flours. This version is vegan, easy and savory. Try making sausage biscuits with DIY Golden Creamy Gravy, page 14.

MAKES ABOUT 10 BISCUITS

1 cup (237 ml) soy milk (or other nondairy milk and leave out the vinegar)

1 teaspoon apple cider vinegar

2 cups (242 grams) whole-wheat pastry flour (*use gluten-free all-purpose baking mix)

1 tablespoon (11 g) baking powder

1 teaspoon ground rosemary (or 1 tablespoon [2.5 g] minced fresh rosemary)

1 teaspoon salt

½ teaspoon ground black pepper

½ cup (90 g) canned pumpkin purée (can substitute sweet potato or butternut squash purée)

2 tablespoons (29 g) coconut oil

Preheat the oven to 425°F (218°C). Oil a large baking sheet.

Whisk the soy milk and vinegar and set aside. While it stands, it will curdle and thicken, creating a vegan buttermilk substitute. (This only works with soy milk. If you use a nut milk or coconut milk, it will not thicken but the recipe will still work.)

Measure the flour into a blender or food processor. Process until the flour is finely ground. This is an important step, because grinding the flour makes the biscuits lighter and fluffier.

Pour the flour into a medium-sized mixing bowl. Add the baking powder, rosemary, salt and pepper. Cut in the pumpkin purée and coconut oil with a pastry cutter or two knives.

Mix the soy milk into the flour mixture. The dough will be sticky, which will create extra-moist biscuits.

Using a large cookie scoop or measuring cup, scoop ¼ cup (60 ml) portions of the dough onto the baking sheet.

Bake until the bottoms are medium brown, about 10 minutes.

Per serving: Calories 123.4, protein 2.7 g, total fat 3.6 g, carbohydrates 20.9 g, sodium 114.5 mg, fiber 3.8 g

VEGGIE QUINOA DROP BISCUITS

• *gluten-free option** • *soy-free*

People in the South love their biscuits, and I am no exception. These biscuits are a little healthier than the usual, and the perfect way to use up that leftover quinoa in your refrigerator. They have the added bonus of containing a few greens, too.

MAKES ABOUT 12 BISCUITS

¾ cup (177 ml) soy milk (or other nondairy milk and leave out the vinegar)

1½ teaspoons (7 ml) apple cider vinegar or white vinegar

1 tablespoon (15 ml) olive oil or broth

½ cup (55 g) finely grated carrot

1½ cups (100 g) finely minced kale or other green

1 cup (185 g) cooked quinoa

2 cups (240 g) whole-wheat pastry flour (*use a gluten-free all-purpose flour)

2 teaspoons (7.5 g) baking powder

½ teaspoon baking soda

½ teaspoon salt

½ cup (112 g) vegan butter, shortening or refined coconut oil

TIP: Try using this recipe to use up other cooked grains such as millet or rice.

Preheat the oven to 350°F (177°C). Whisk the soy milk and vinegar and set aside. While it stands, it will curdle and thicken, creating a vegan buttermilk substitute. (This only works with soy milk. If you use a nut milk or coconut milk, it will not thicken but the recipe will still work.)

Heat the olive oil or broth in a sauté pan over medium heat and add the kale. Sauté for 1 to 3 minutes or until it turns bright green. Pour into a large bowl with the carrots and quinoa. Set aside.

To a food processor, add the whole-wheat pastry flour and process for about 2 minutes to make it finer and the biscuit a little lighter. Add baking powder, baking soda and salt and process for about 1 minute.

Next, add the vegan butter or shortening to the food processor ⅛ of a cup (28 g) at a time and pulse for 30 seconds to a minute after each addition. The mixture will start to look like coarse cornmeal. If there are a few teaspoon-sized lumps of butter, don't worry—they will mix in later.

Pour the flour mixture into the large bowl with the veggies, quinoa and soy milk-vinegar mixture. Mix well with a wooden spoon to spread the veggies throughout and smash up any butter pieces that remain.

Grease two cookie sheets or line them with parchment paper. Using a large scoop (about ¼ cup [60 ml]), form about 12 biscuits. They will be domed from the scoop; if you wish, flatten them with the palm of your hand. They will not spread out during cooking.

Cook for 13 to 17 minutes, or until they turn light brown on the bottoms. Eat as is, covered with gravy or in the middle of your favorite meatless stew or chili.

Per biscuit with oil: Calories 212.4, protein 4.4 g, total fat 9.9 g, carbohydrates 26.5 g, sodium 115.1 mg, fiber 4.2 g

ZUCCHINI MASALA FRIES

• *gluten-free* • *soy-free*

There's always too much zucchini in my summer CSA, and often even more in my small garden, too. Once you get tired of zucchini noodles, make a few batches of these zucchini fries. They are easy to whip up, and the Indian spices will add some zing to your next dinner party.

SERVES 4

4 small or 2 large zucchinis, cut into sticks approximately ½" x 2½" (1.3 x 6.3 cm)

1 tablespoon (15 ml) olive oil

2 teaspoons (6.3 g) brown rice flour (or any flour you have on hand)

1 teaspoon garam masala

1 teaspoon cumin

Salt and pepper

Preheat the oven to 350°F (177°C) and line two baking sheets with parchment paper.

Toss the zucchini and olive oil together in a bowl.

Mix the flour, garam masala and cumin together well, then add it to the zucchini. Using your hands or a wooden spoon, mix until the spice mixture is stuck to the zucchini.

Spread out the zucchinis on the baking sheets, then lightly sprinkle them with salt and pepper. Bake for 10 to 15 minutes, until tender but not limp.

Per serving with oil: Calories 61.6, protein 2.1 g, total fat 3.7 g, carbohydrates 6.7 g, sodium 0.2 mg, fiber 0.0 g

TIP: Make a creamy dip by combining unsweetened vegan yogurt or Cashew Sour Cream (page 22) with chopped cilantro and a little coriander and cumin.

BAKED CRISPY BREADED GREEN BEANS

• *gluten-free option** • *soy-free* • *oil-free option***

This is a treat you can feel good about serving. Deep-fried green beans made this dish popular, but yours will be baked after being coated in bread crumbs. Best part: the sriracha mayo you dip them in! These are great as a side or a party snack.

SERVES 4

1 pound (453 g) green beans with the stem end snapped off

1 tablespoon (15 ml) olive oil

1 cup (45 g) bread crumbs (*use gluten-free)

½ teaspoon salt

½ teaspoon granulated garlic

Sriracha Mayo Dip (page 169), to serve

Preheat the oven to 400°F (204°C). Line two cookie sheets with parchment paper.

Toss the green beans and olive oil in a mixing bowl. In a separate large mixing bowl, combine the bread crumbs, salt and garlic.

Put a handful (or tong-ful) of oiled green beans into the bread crumbs and toss to coat. You can use a wooden spoon or tongs to mix the beans around in the crumbs. A light coating will stick to each green bean. ("Light coating" means there will be some uncoated spaces on the beans.)

Spread out the beans in a single layer on the baking sheets.

Bake for 13 to 16 minutes, depending on the thickness of the beans. Test one for doneness: it shouldn't taste raw, but it shouldn't be limp, either.

The beans won't turn dark brown, but if you'd like them to, you can broil them for a couple of minutes.

Serve with Sriracha Mayo Dip.

Per serving with oil: Calories 171.6, protein 5.7 g, total fat 4.9 g, carbohydrates 27.5 g, sodium 204.4 mg, fiber 5.1 g

TIP: **Spicy Oil-Free Version: Use a mixture of 1 tablespoon (15 ml) mustard and ½ tablespoon (7.5 ml) apple cider vinegar in place of the olive oil. You won't need the Sriracha Mayo Dip because the beans will be spicy all by themselves. Try some vegan yogurt on the side to cool things down.

SRIRACHA MAYO DIP

MAKES A LITTLE OVER ¼ CUP (59 ML)

¼ cup (60 g) vegan mayo, or Cashew Sour Cream (page 22) or Tofu Sour Cream (page 23)

½ teaspoon to 1 tablespoon (0.25 ml to 15 ml) sriracha, to taste

Mix the mayo and sriracha in a bowl. Serve in individual dipping bowls.

DREAMY GREENS

• *gluten-free*   • *soy-free*   • *oil-free option**

If you have ever belonged to a winter or spring CSA, you know what it's like to get a mountain of greens every week. You can make only so many green smoothies before you're looking for other places to use them up. No matter how tired of greens you are, I promise that these rich greens with coconut milk and nutmeg will still seem special. Be sure to try the Indian spice option, too!

SERVES 4

1 to 2 tablespoons (15-30 ml) olive oil (*sauté in water instead)

½ cup (80 g) chopped onion

2 cloves garlic, minced

6 tightly packed cups (200 g) cleaned and torn fresh greens (see note below**)

½ cup (120 ml) coconut milk

¼ teaspoon nutmeg

¼ teaspoon salt

⅛ teaspoon pepper

1 teaspoon tapioca or cornstarch (optional)

Heat the oil in a soup pot over medium heat. Add the onion and sauté for about 5 minute or until translucent. Add the garlic and sauté a minute or two more.

Add the greens 2 cups (67 g) at a time as they cook down. Once they have all been added and wilted, stir in the coconut milk, nutmeg, salt and pepper.

If you'd like to thicken the sauce, spoon out a tablespoon (15 ml) of liquid from the greens and mix in the starch of your choice. Add the mixture back to the greens and cook until thickened.

**Note: Greens can range from mild to bitter. If you aren't sure about what you have, take a bite of it raw. Also, the weight of greens varies by type. Metric users, measure by volume if possible.

Per serving with oil: Calories 156.7, protein 3.5 g, total fat 4.0 g, carbohydrates 15.6 g, sodium 1474.5 mg, fiber 6.4 g

TIP: Make this into a whole meal by doubling the recipe, replacing the nutmeg with garam masala and adding a can of chickpeas or seared tofu for an Indian saag.

ANN'S SWEET POTATO FRIES WITH PARSLEY, GARLIC AND LEMON ZEST

• gluten-free • soy-free • oil-free option*

Ann Oliverio is the force behind the Virtual Vegan Potluck. She also makes tasty food and is the photographer for this book. About this recipe, she says, "Just look at those bright orange babies dotted with flecks of fresh green, dabs of garlic and zingy lemon—all glistening with one of my current favorite muses: coconut oil." Make sure to check out her new cookbook *Crave, Eat, Heal*.

SERVES 4

1 very large sweet potato, peeled and cut into long strips (like fries)

½ tablespoon (7 g) virgin coconut oil

1 clove garlic, minced

¼ cup (15 g) parsley, minced

Zest of 1 lemon, minced

Preheat oven to 425°F (218°C) and line a baking sheet with parchment paper. Spread sweet potato slices onto pan in a single layer and bake for about 15 minutes.

Turn slices and continue to bake until they are soft and beginning to brown, about 5 to 10 minutes more.

Just before the fries are done, heat the coconut oil over medium heat and sauté the garlic in the oil until fragrant. Add the fries to the pan and stir, coating them with the oil and garlic.

Remove pan from the heat and stir in the parsley and lemon zest.

Per serving with oil: Calories 50.2, protein 0.6 g, total fat 1.9 g, carbohydrates 8.1 g, sodium 4.4 mg, fiber 1.0 g

TIP: *Mary Banker, one of my new testers, modified this recipe by tossing the fries in lemon juice in place of the coconut oil. It's a great oil-free option!

SPICY CREAMED CORN

• *gluten-free* • *soy-free* • *no oil added*

Cheryl, my picky eater, loves creamed corn. This is a veganized and spiced-up version of her old favorite. It's great a side dish and a great dip with tortilla chips. I like to double the recipe and keep it warm in a slow cooker for parties.

SERVES 4

½ cup (113 g) cashews

½ cup (118 ml) water

½ cup (74.5 g) chopped bell pepper

1 tablespoon (11 g) chopped green chilies (or minced jalapeños for extra heat)

1 teaspoon cumin

½ teaspoon smoked paprika

½ teaspoon chili powder

½ teaspoon chipotle powder (optional)

¼ teaspoon jalapeño powder (optional)

2 cups (332 g) corn kernels

1 teaspoon oregano

¼ teaspoon liquid smoke

Salt, to taste

Soak the cashews in the water for 2 hours if you have a high-speed blender, or overnight if you don't. Blend until smooth. The mixture will be thick like cream. Set aside.

Heat a sauté pan over medium heat and add the bell pepper, green chilies, cumin, smoked paprika, chili powder and the additional chipotle and jalapeño powder, if using. Cook until the spices are fragrant and the bell peppers soften, about 3 minutes.

Stir in the cashew mixture, corn, oregano and liquid smoke and cook until the corn kernels are tender. Salt to taste and serve.

Per serving: Calories 86.0, protein 2.2 g, total fat 6.5 g, carbohydrates 5.6 g, sodium 55.6 mg, fiber 0.3 g

TIP: You probably have chipotle powder in your spice drawer, but you might not have jalapeño powder. I like to keep it so I don't have to run to the store for a fresh jalapeño. Try sprinkling it with a little salt over cooked beans—it's amazing!

DESSERTS AND DRINKS

You can still treat yourself to dessert even if you want to make easy meals. You won't find any fancy iced cakes in here, but you will find Maple Walnut Blondies (page 180), a brownie recipe with avocado (page 179), spice cake (page 188) and more. There's even a recipe for Orange Chocolate Mousse Parfait (page 187) that takes very little effort because it's your blender or food processor doing all the work.

My friend Jenni Field, of PastryChefOnline.com, contributed an amazing wine granita (page 184) that's perfect for a summer dinner on the deck, plus an apple crisp (page 191) that uses your food processor to cut down on prep time.

Two of my favorite frozen drinks are in this chapter. My Sweet Potato Spice Frozen Latte (page 192) is made with a coffee concentrate that I also show you how to make. These were life-changing for me, keeping me out of the coffeehouse line on the way to work. The Salted Caramel No-Ice-Cream Milk Shake (page 196) works as a dessert or snack, and you can add some coffee to it, too.

SURPRISE WALNUT BROWNIES

• *gluten-free option** • *soy-free* • *no oil added*

Brownies with walnuts are Cheryl's most-requested treat. These are rich without any added oil. The secret is mashed avocado in place of the traditional oil. These are rich and fudgy and are quick to make. The hardest part is waiting until they are ready to eat.

MAKES 12 BROWNIES

2 tablespoons (14 g) ground flaxseed mixed with 4 tablespoons (56 ml) warm water

2 medium avocados

1 cup (145 g) coconut sugar or brown sugar

1 teaspoon vanilla

½ teaspoon salt

1¼ cups (150 g) whole-wheat pastry flour (*use gluten-free baking mix)

½ cup (43 g) baking cocoa

½ teaspoon baking powder

1 cup (117 g) walnuts (or nut of your choice)

Preheat oven to 350°F (177°C). Prepare an 8" x 8" (20 x 20 cm) square baking pan by covering with parchment paper. It's okay if it bunches up in the corners. If it comes up a bit over the top of the pan, it'll help you remove the brownies.

Add the flaxseed mixture, avocado, sugar, vanilla and salt to your food processor and process until silky smooth.

Combine the flour, cocoa and baking powder in a mixing bowl. Stir in the avocado mixture until you have a thick batter. Add the walnuts, mix, then scrape into the prepared pan.

Spread the batter as evenly as you can in the prepared pan. Bake for 30 to 35 minutes. You want to slightly underbake these to keep the fudgelike texture, so pull them out before a fork comes out of the middle completely dry.

Per brownie: Calories 212.6, protein 5.0 g, total fat 11.7 g, carbohydrates 31.9 g, sodium 26.1 mg, fiber 4.7 g

TIP: Allergic to nuts? Swap them for chocolate chips for extra-chocolaty brownies.

MY FAVORITE MAPLE WALNUT BLONDIES

• gluten-free option* • soy-free • oil-free option**

Everyone needs a quick and easy bar cookie recipe up their sleeve, and this is mine. They are great any time of year, but the combination of maple flavor with walnuts seems perfect for fall. Make these for your next celebration, or bring them to a potluck. While not overly sweet, they are impossibly fudgelike, and no one will ever guess they're vegan.

MAKES 12 BLONDIES

2 tablespoons (14 g) ground flaxseed mixed with 4 tablespoons (56 ml) warm water

¼ cup (54 g) coconut oil, melted (**use pumpkin purée)

¾ cup (108 g) coconut sugar or brown sugar

¼ cup (60 ml) maple syrup

1 teaspoon vanilla

1 teaspoon salt

1 cup (132 g) whole-wheat pastry flour (*use gluten-free baking mix)

½ cup (50 g) walnuts (or nut of your choice)

Preheat oven to 350°F (177°C). Prepare an 8" x 8" (20 x 20 cm) square baking pan by covering with parchment paper. It's okay if it bunches up in the corners. If it comes up a bit over the top of the pan, it'll help you remove the blondies.

Add the flaxseed mixture, oil, sugar, maple syrup, vanilla and salt to your stand mixer and mix well. (Note: you can certainly do this in a bowl, by hand, if you don't have a mixer.)

Add the flour about ⅓ cup (42 g) at a time and mix until just incorporated. When you've added the full cup of flour, the batter will be extra thick.

Add the walnuts, mix, then scrape into the prepared pan.

Spread the batter as evenly as you can in the prepared pan. Bake for 25 to 35 minutes. You want to slightly underbake these to keep the fudgelike texture, so pull them out before a fork comes out of the middle completely dry.

Per blondie with oil: Calories 171.4, protein 2.1 g, total fat 8.9 g, carbohydrates 25.6 g, sodium 4.9 mg, fiber 2.2 g

TIP: Switch out the nuts for chocolate chips if you can't live without chocolate in your blondies.

PECAN COCONUT CHOCOLATE CHIP BARS

• *gluten-free option** • *soy-free* • *oil-free option***

When I need something sweet in a hurry, I like to make these bar cookies. Cheryl loves all things chocolate, so I throw in chocolate chips for her and coconut and pecan for me. I'm not sure how much time making bars saves from making individual cookies, but I certainly feel like there's less effort involved!

MAKES 12 BARS

2 tablespoons (14 g) ground flaxseed mixed with 4 tablespoons (56 ml) warm water

½ cup (110 g) melted coconut oil (**use equal amount of applesauce or pumpkin purée)

½ cup (110 g) brown or coconut sugar

¼ cup (60 ml) nondairy milk

1 teaspoon vanilla

½ teaspoon salt

1¼ cups (150 g) whole-wheat pastry flour (*use gluten-free baking blend)

½ teaspoon baking soda

½ cup (50 g) pecans

¼ cup (46.5 g) unsweetened shredded coconut

½ cup (90 g) chocolate chips (I love using the mini ones)

Preheat oven to 350°F (177°C). Prepare an 8" x 8" (20 x 20 cm) square baking pan by covering with parchment paper. It's okay if it bunches up in the corners.

Add the flaxseed mixture, oil, sugar, milk, vanilla and salt to your stand mixer and mix well. (You can certainly do this in a bowl, by hand, if you don't have a mixer.)

Mix the baking soda and flour. Add about ⅓ cup (42 g) of the flour mixture at a time and mix until just incorporated. When you've added all of the flour, the batter will be thick.

Add the pecans, coconut and chocolate chips and mix until incorporated.

Spread the batter as evenly as you can in the prepared pan. Bake for 20 to 25 minutes, or until a fork comes out of the middle completely dry.

Per bar with oil: Calories 275.5, protein 2.7 g, total fat 19.1 g, carbohydrates 26.5 g, sodium 71.6 mg, fiber 9.9 g

TIP: I use pecans because I live in the South, where they're cheap. It also doesn't hurt that Cheryl gets two large bags of them free every year where she works. Feel free to substitute any nut you have in the pantry.

JENNI FIELD'S RIESLING GRANITA

• *gluten-free* • *soy-free* • *no oil added*

My friend Jenni is the talented blogger behind PastryChefOnline.com and this easy Riesling granita. It's a wonderful, icy-cold, winey-sweet dish (in Jenni's words). You do need to make it the night before you serve it, but hands-on time is minimal. It's all worth it when you get to eat frozen wine for dessert!

SERVES 4

2¼ cups (532 ml) water

Slightly less than 1 cup (6 oz [170 g]) sugar

⅛ teaspoon salt

1 (750 ml) bottle sweet Riesling

Approximately ¼ to ⅓ cup (60 to 78 ml) lemon juice, to taste

Heat the water and dissolve the sugar and salt in it. It doesn't have to boil—you just want the salt and sugar crystals to dissolve. Combine with the wine and lemon juice. Taste. It should be sweet and winey and have a nice tang from the lemon juice.

Pour into a shallow 9" x 9" (23 x 23 cm) pan, wrap with plastic wrap, and freeze overnight. One of the many wonderful things about this granita is that, because of the alcohol in it, it doesn't freeze superfirm. When you're ready to serve, just remove from the freezer and scrape with a fork. You will end up with very pale golden shards of ice wine.

You can make this with wine, too.

Per serving: Calories 329.3, protein 0.1 g, total fat 0.0 g, carbohydrates 51.3 g, sodium 0.2 mg, fiber 0.1 g

TIP: Not all wines are vegan! Barnivore.com is a website that has a list of what's vegan and what's not. I recommend that you download their mobile app so you can check while you're in the store in front of the wine display.

ORANGE CHOCOLATE MOUSSE PARFAIT

• *gluten-free*

This is my go-to dessert for last-minute dinners I find myself hosting. It takes minutes to pull together, and it tastes like it took hours. It is very rich and is wonderful between layers of cookie crumbs. Use whatever liqueur you like or happen to have. You can also make this without alcohol and use 1 teaspoon of your favorite flavor extract instead.

SERVES 6

1 (12.3 oz [349 g]) package silken tofu

½ cup (113 g) sweetened chocolate chips

2 tablespoons (30 ml) Grand Marnier or other liqueur of your choice

1 cup (80 g) crushed vegan chocolate or vanilla cookies

Purée the tofu in a food processor until silky smooth, stopping a few times to scrape down the sides.

Melt chocolate chips on the stove top in a double boiler, or in the microwave for 30 to 45 seconds. Add melted chocolate and liqueur to the food processor and process until thoroughly mixed, scraping down the sides as needed.

Layer in small cups or martini glasses. Start with a layer of mousse, then add a layer of cookie, until you have filled the glass. Chill in the refrigerator for at least 1 hour to let it thicken up.

Per serving: Calories 212.1, protein 6.3 g, total fat 9.2 g, carbohydrates 27.8 g, sodium 130.9 mg, fiber 1.9 g

APPLESAUCE SPICE CAKE

• gluten-free option* *• soy-free* *• oil-free option***

My Aunt Bill used to make an applesauce cake around the holidays, and it was my favorite. No icing, no fuss—just a mouthful of flavor. This cake has the same balance of spices: cinnamon and cloves with hints of ginger and allspice. It's a step away from gingerbread—you could even add more ginger if you'd like.

MAKES 10 SERVINGS

WET INGREDIENTS

1 cup (255 g) applesauce

⅓ cup (79 ml) oil (**substitute ⅔ cup [165 g] applesauce or pumpkin purée)

1 tablespoon (15 ml) apple cider vinegar or white vinegar

DRY INGREDIENTS

2 cups (240 g) whole-wheat pastry flour (*use a gluten-free baking mix)

1 cup (192 g) coconut sugar

1½ teaspoons (7 g) cinnamon

1 teaspoon baking soda

1 teaspoon salt

¾ teaspoon ground ginger

¾ teaspoon allspice

¼ teaspoon plus ⅛ teaspoon ground cloves

Preheat the oven to 350°F (177°C) and oil a tall 9" (23 cm) cake pan.

Mix the wet ingredients together in a measuring cup. Mix the dry ones together in a medium-sized bowl.

Add the wet ingredients to the dry until just combined.

Scrape out the batter into the cake pan and bake until a fork comes out clean in the middle, about 45 minutes.

Per serving: Calories 242.6, protein 3.2 g, total fat 8.0 g, carbohydrates 42.8 g, sodium 0.8 mg, fiber 3.5 g

TIP: This cake rises because of the chemical reaction of baking soda and vinegar. There isn't an egg substitute because this recipe is based on a cake that was popular in the Depression, when eggs were scarce.

JENNI'S BOOZY SHREDDED APPLE CRISP

• *gluten-free option** • *soy-free*

I try to get together as often as possible with my friend Jenni of PastryChefOnline.com. I usually manage to convince her to make and bring a few vegan goodies that I can share with my own readers. The shredded apples cook down to an almost jamlike consistency, and the liqueurs add a rich flavor that makes this crisp holiday worthy.

SERVES 12

FOR THE APPLE MIXTURE

6 sweet-tart apples, such as Golden Delicious or Braeburn (peeling optional)

2 tablespoons (30 ml) Grand Marnier or other orange brandy

2 tablespoons (30 ml) Frangelico or other hazelnut liqueur

1 tablespoon (9 g) sugar (brown or coconut sugar)

1 tablespoon (8 g) tapioca starch (or cornstarch or flour), optional, but will help to thicken the mixture

¼ teaspoon cinnamon

¼ teaspoon nutmeg

Pinch of allspice

Healthy pinch of salt

FOR THE STREUSEL

¾ cup (109 g) dark brown sugar

½ cup (63 g) unbleached all-purpose flour (or whole-wheat pastry flour or *gluten-free baking mix)

½ cup (78 g) rolled oats (*make sure they are marked "gluten-free")

¼ cup (29 g) toasted hazelnuts, finely chopped (optional but lovely)

Healthy pinch of salt

¼ teaspoon cinnamon

¼ teaspoon nutmeg

Pinch of allspice

½ cup (105 g) coconut oil

Preheat the oven to 350°F (177°C). Oil a 9" x 13" (23 x 33 cm) baking pan and set aside.

FOR THE APPLE MIXTURE

Wash the apples well and peel them. If you don't want to peel them, dip them in boiling water for about 10 seconds to break down the wax they're coated in. Remove from the water and scrub under running water.

Quarter each apple, cut out the core and shred, either by hand or with your food processor's coarse shredding disc. Place the shredded apples in the prepared baking pan, then mix in the Grand Marnier, Frangelico and sugar. Add the starch (if using) and the remaining ingredients and toss to combine.

FOR THE STREUSEL

Combine all the streusel ingredients in a bowl. Cut in the coconut oil with your fingers or a pastry cutter until the mixture is well-blended and no longer floury.

Spread the streusel evenly over the apples and bake for 45 minutes to an hour, or until the streusel is golden brown and the apples are bubbling all over.

Let cool for at least a few minutes before serving.

Per serving: Calories 177.8, protein 1.5 g, total fat 6.4 g, carbohydrates 29.9 g, sodium 1.3 mg, fiber 2.8 g

TIP: Jenni says, "You can add a dollop of vegan ice cream (coconut milk-based would work well) or whipped coconut cream to make it extra decadent. Enjoy!"

SWEET POTATO SPICE FROZEN LATTE

• *gluten-free* • *soy-free* • *no added oil*

Pumpkin spice has a cult following. It's now in everything fall-themed, from drinks to body lotions. Why not break out of the pumpkin spice latte mold and give this delicious sweet potato drink a chance to be your new favorite?

SERVES 2

1¼ cups (312 ml) nondairy milk

¼ cup (64 g) sweet potato purée

¼ cup (63 ml) coffee concentrate (page 195)

½ teaspoon cinnamon

¼ teaspoon cardamom

⅛ teaspoon allspice

⅛ teaspoon nutmeg

pinch ground cloves

Sweetener of choice, to taste

⅛ teaspoon xanthan gum or 1 teaspoon pectin or 1½ teaspoons (7 g) ground chia seeds

2 cups (43 g) ice

Add the milk, sweet potato, coffee and spices to your blender. Blend until they're combined well and there are no lumps of potato.

Add the xanthan gum (or pectin or chia seeds) and blend. This ingredient will keep the others from separating. Now taste and add sweetener, adjusting as needed. Remember, this is a concentrated flavor, so it needs to be a little sweeter now to be just right with ice.

Add the ice. Depending on how powerful your blender is, you may have to add it ½ cup (120 g) at a time.

Add more nondairy milk if it's too thick or more ice if it's too thin.

Per serving: Calories 58.4, protein 1.4 g, total fat 2.2 g, carbohydrates 9.3 g, sodium 139.1 mg, fiber 1.3 g

TIPS: Don't want coffee in your Sweet Potato Spice Frozen Latte? Leave it out and add a touch more nondairy milk, or substitute tea for a creamy drink that you can't get at a coffeehouse!

Lots of thickening options! If you don't have xanthan gum, pectin or chia seeds, add about half of a large frozen banana.

One of my lovely testers, Mary Banker, came up with the ground chia. Chia is less expensive than xanthan gum and adds a nutritional boost.

DIY COFFEE CONCENTRATE

Coffee concentrate is dirt cheap, and you get to make it with the roast you like best. The hands-on time to make it is about 5 minutes—maybe 10 if you grind your own beans—and it keeps in the refrigerator for about 2 weeks.

2 tablespoons (11 g) ground coffee per 1 cup (237 ml) your French press holds

Water to fill French press

Add the ground coffee to your French press.

Add water until the mixture is about a finger's width below the pour spout. Carefully place the filter or plunger so that it is just on top of the grounds, keeping them under the water. Let sit overnight in the refrigerator.

In the morning, gently press down the plunger to push the coffee grounds to the bottom. Pour into your favorite pitcher (with a lid) or mason jar(s) and store in the refrigerator.

TIP: Use more ground coffee per cup of water to make a stronger concentrate.

SALTED CARAMEL NO-ICE-CREAM MILK SHAKE

• *gluten-free* • *soy-free* • *no oil added*

In the summer, I get cravings for a frosty drink to cool myself down. This one is great because it doesn't require ice cream, but it's thick and rich anyway. Trust me; the dates make it taste just like caramel. Use this recipe as a template for other flavored no-ice-cream shakes.

SERVES 2

1 cup (243 ml) vanilla nondairy milk

4 dates, soaked for 15 minutes and drained

½ teaspoon vanilla

Sweetener, optional to taste

⅛ teaspoon xanthan gum or 1 teaspoon pectin or 1½ teaspoons (7 g) ground chia seeds

2 cups (43 g) ice

Add the nondairy milk and dates to your blender. If you have a high-speed blender, you can skip soaking the dates, but it will be smoother if you do. Blend until smooth.

Add the vanilla, sweetener and xanthan gum and blend again. Make sure the xanthan gum gets mixed in and doesn't just stick to the side of the pitcher.

Add the ice. Depending on how powerful your blender is, you may have to add it ½ cup (120 g) at a time.

Per serving: Calories 100.7, protein 0.9 g, total fat 1.8 g, carbohydrates 21.6 g, sodium 90.4 mg, fiber 1.8 g

TIPS: Lots of thickening options! If you don't have xanthan gum, pectin or chia seeds, add about half of a large frozen banana.

Make yours a frozen caramel coffee by using ¼ cup (59 ml) coffee concentrate and 1½ cups (355 ml) nondairy milk. You can even throw in a tablespoon (8 g) of cocoa powder to make it a caramel mocha! Change it to a holiday shake by adding a tablespoon or two (9-18 g) of cocoa and a few drops of peppermint extract. Try different extracts and add fruit, too. I've been making strawberry shakes with this recipe!

RESOURCES

STOCKING YOUR PANTRY

A well-stocked pantry is your best insurance for an easy meal. If you're in a pinch, a drained and rinsed can of beans tossed with some cooked pasta and a little sauce can be a lifesaver. Never underestimate what a well-stocked pantry can do for you.

Having ingredients available means you'll spend less eating out at the last minute and that you'll be eating healthier foods. If you are on a tight budget, just start with some flour, sweetener, olive oil, brown rice, pasta and a few cans of beans and tomatoes.

My idea of a well-stocked pantry:

- agave nectar
- almonds
- applesauce
- brown rice
- brown rice flour
- bulgur
- canned and dry beans (black, pinto, kidney, chickpea, white beans)
- canned crushed tomatoes (or frozen)
- canned diced tomatoes (or frozen)
- cans of pumpkin or butternut squash purée (Tip: After the holidays, you can find organic very cheaply)

- cashews (for a quick cashew cream)
- coconut oil
- coconut sugar or brown sugar
- dried pasta (assorted types such as macaroni, shapes and spaghetti)
- lemons or refrigerated lemon juice
- maple syrup
- millet
- nondairy milk (soy, almond, rice, coconut, etc.—unsweetened, both plain and vanilla)
- olive oil

- olives
- peanuts
- premade pasta sauce
- quinoa
- rolled oats
- shelf-stable silken tofu
- tomato paste
- tortillas (corn and flour—these can also be kept in the freezer)
- walnuts
- whole-wheat and/or brown rice couscous
- whole-wheat pastry flour

HERBS, SPICES AND CONDIMENTS

You don't need to have all of the ones in this book to start cooking. Instead, add a new one to your collection every week or month.

Remember that you can get tiny amounts of dried herbs and spices in bulk at Whole Foods Market or your local co-op. SavorySpiceShop.com and MySpiceSage.com also sell bulk spices, but you have to buy at least 1 ounce there.

If you are on a tight budget, start with salt, pepper, nutritional yeast, bay leaves, liquid smoke, chili powder, garlic powder, basil and oregano.

- allspice
- apple cider vinegar
- balsamic vinegar
- basil
- bay leaves
- black pepper
- DIY Cajun Seasoning Blend (recipe on page 30)
- cardamom
- cayenne powder
- chili garlic paste
- chili powder
- cinnamon
- cloves
- coriander (ground)
- cornstarch (use organic or substitute tapioca starch)
- cumin (ground and seed)
- garam
- garlic (granulated or powder and fresh)
- ginger (ground and fresh)
- liquid smoke (any flavor)
- marjoram (similar to oregano; you can substitute one for the other)
- nutmeg
- nutritional yeast
- onion powder
- oregano
- paprika (regular and smoked)
- red pepper flakes
- rice wine vinegar
- rosemary
- sage (rubbed)
- salt
- sesame oil
- sriracha chili sauce
- soy sauce (gluten-free if you need; substitute coconut aminos for soy- and gluten-free)
- Tabasco (or other vinegar-based hot sauce)
- tahini
- thyme
- turmeric
- vanilla extract
- vegan mayo (or substitute Cashew Sour Cream, page 22, or Tofu Sour Cream, page 23)

COOKING METHODS

Many of the recipes have both a stove top and a slow cooker cooking method. If you follow my blog, HealthySlowCooking.com, or you have one of my slow cooker cookbooks, you know I love the hands-off ease that they add to my routine.

You do not need a slow cooker to make any of the recipes in this book, but I highly recommend adding one to your kitchen if you don't have one already. An inexpensive 4-quart (4-L) slow cooker can make dry beans from scratch and cook up a soup or stew when you come home for dinner.

APPLIANCES

Besides a slow cooker, I do use a few appliances in some of the recipes. The most-often used are a food processor, a regular blender and an immersion blender.

TYPICAL VEGAN INGREDIENTS

If you're new to eating vegan, there may be a few ingredients in this book that are new to you. Here's a rundown that explains what they are and where you can buy them.

Butler's Soy Curls are a product from the Pacific Northwest. They are soybeans that have been smashed and dried. They have a meaty texture when reconstituted and not much flavor on their own. That said, they are a perfect base for your favorite sauces, and they make a wonderful BBQ sandwich. If you are not in the northwest, you'll need to order them online. Amazon has them.

Cauliflower, mushrooms and shredded sweet potatoes show up in many recipes where you might expect a meat substitute. Cauliflower is great for veganizing a family fish or chicken recipe; portabella mushrooms give an umami flavor and chewy texture that are a good replacement for beef; and shredded sweet potatoes are great for veganizing a shredded meat recipe.

Chickpeas are my default choice for a meat substitute like Beyond Meat or a soy product like tempeh. Of all the beans, chickpeas retain their shape after long cooking times and give some of that toothsome feel you would expect.

Kala Namak is also known as "black salt" even though it's pink. That's because the outside of the rock is black, but by the time it's in a jar we only see the insides. It's used often in vegan recipes to mimic the taste of eggs. It's high in sulfur, which gives it that eggy taste and smell. It turns a plain tofu scramble into something amazing. Because it's used in Indian food quite often, you can find it cheaply at Indian markets. But don't worry if there isn't any in your area; you can order it online at MySpiceSage.com, at SavorySpiceShop.com or on Amazon.

Liquid smoke and smoked paprika add that smoky flavor. Some people are under the misconception that liquid smoke isn't natural, but it's actually the condensation from real wood being burned, and almost all brands do not contain chemicals. Check labels to make sure you are getting the natural kind. It can be found in all groceries in the South in the condiment section, and you can easily order it online.

Nondairy cream substitutes are an easy way to amp up the richness of a recipe. I have recipes for cashew and tofu sour cream that thicken as well. There's a recipe for pumpkin cashew cheese that's amazing on your morning bagel. You can also buy premade versions at your local natural food store and in some groceries. Kite Hill has an amazing vegan cream cheese.

Nondairy milks are popular far beyond the vegan community and can be found in most regular groceries. They have an array of bases such as soy, almond, coconut, cashew, oat and hemp; and more varieties keep coming. I call for unsweetened nondairy milk in savory dishes because they add richness without sweetness. You can use plain milk if you can't find unsweetened, but it will add a slight sweetness even to savory dishes.

Nutritional Yeast is not the same as brewer's yeast or baking yeast, so be sure not to mix them up. Nutritional yeast is full of umami flavor and B vitamins. If you can't find it in a bulk bin at a Whole Foods Market or co-op near you, try ordering online from Bob's Red Mill or Amazon. It's used in recipes that traditionally have cheese in them, to mimic that cheesy flavor. It's used as an addition to soups and stews—even gravies. It's also great as a popcorn topping.

Seitan is made from wheat gluten. You can find seitan premade in the refrigerated section of most natural foods stores. You can also easily order vital wheat gluten online and make your own from scratch.

Soy Curls, Beyond Meat, Gardein and other meat substitutes contain soy. Soy Curls and Beyond Meat are both gluten-free, and some of the new Gardein products are gluten-free as well. If you are avoiding gluten and/or soy, always read labels carefully, since brands will often change their formulas.

Sometimes having an easy substitution for veganizing your pre-vegan recipes can make the transition easier. It also helps non-vegans cook for us. I live with a non-vegan; and adding in Soy Curls, Beyond Meat and Gardein once or twice a week makes it easier for her to eat meatless at home. Some other brands I use are Lightlife and Gimme Lean; there will probably be even more by the time this book is in print. Read their ingredient lists to see whether they fit into your eating plan.

As of this writing, you can get Gardein in the freezer section of most major grocery stores. It and Beyond Meat are even in the freezer section in Target. With luck, this trend will continue so that they are easier to find near you.

Spices elevate a plain dish. There are a few in this book that you may not yet have in your cabinet. I recommend that you buy spices in bulk stores while trying them out because you can buy as little as a tablespoon. You can usually find bulk spices at natural foods stores. Some of the most-used spices in the book are cumin (ground and seeds), chili powder, garam masala, ground coriander and turmeric. Garam masala is a blend of Indian spices that is more interesting and flavorful than typical curry powder, but you can substitute curry powder in a pinch. See the spice list on page 199 for a complete list of those used in this book.

Tempeh is made from soybeans that have been cut in half and cultured. It has a firm bite; in chunks, it can be substituted for chicken in some of your non-vegan recipes. You can also crumble it up and use it where you'd use mince. Some people find tempeh a bit bitter. If you're one of them, try steaming it for 10 minutes before you use it in your recipe. Another alternative is to try different brands; maybe a local maker has one that isn't bitter.

Some people who avoid many soy products will eat fermented ones like tempeh and miso. If you are allergic, however, you should not eat even those.

Tofu is made from soybeans. There are different types of tofu: silken, regular and sprouted. There are even ones that have been baked in a marinade and are ready to eat. You can get most types of tofu in degrees of firmness from soft to extra-firm. Silken tofu has a custard-like texture. Used as is, it works perfectly for puddings. Regular and sprouted tofu usually need to have the water pressed out so they can absorb a marinade, but you can skip this step with extra-firm tofu.

It's all about options. Some people don't like the idea of anything remotely processed, vegan or not. I always offer options in my recipes to suit that preference as well as other dietary needs. So a recipe may call for Beyond Meat or cubed tempeh or cubed seitan or chickpeas. What you use is up to you. Each one will make the dish slightly different, and all will make for a tasty dinner. You can always use one of the vegetables mentioned above as well.

ACKNOWLEDGMENTS

This is my second book with Page Street Publishing, and I love working with Will Kiester and his team even more than I did at first. Lisa and Sally Ekus, my amazing agents, have been wonderfully supportive through the whole process of this book and many other behind-the-scenes projects.

I have so much gratitude for my testers' help and guidance: Rochelle Arvizo, Mary Banker, Debbie Blicher, Julie Cross, Vicki Brett-Gach, Faith Hood, Jessica Ledford, Kim Logan, Ann Oliverio and Anna Pelzer.

Many thanks to Marissa Giambelluca and Debbie Blicher for doing a great editing job. I love Meg Baskis's wonderful layout for this book. As usual, I can't possibly thank Cheryl Purser enough, and you should know that she's the reason that nutritionals make it into my books.

ABOUT THE AUTHOR

Kathy Hester is the author of *OATragous Oatmeals, Vegan Slow Cooking for Two or Just You*, *The Great Vegan Bean Book* and the bestselling *The Vegan Slow Cooker*. She's the blogger behind healthyslowcooking.com, as well as doing freelance recipe development, blogging and online PR for cookbook authors. She lives in Durham, North Carolina with a grown-up picky eater, two quirky dogs and two grumpy cats.

INDEX